# The History of Ukraine and Russia

*The Tangled History That Led to Crisis*

**Marc Miles Vaughn**

## Table of Contents

# Introduction: Reflections from 2022

*"Chess is war over the board. The object is to crush the opponent's mind." –Bobby Fisher*

Clambering around the bombed ruins and smoking carcasses of Russian tanks in Lukyanivka, UN officials and global media reporters are trying to make sense of Russia's "four-day special military operation" in Ukraine. As I write, the Russian forces have been driven back from Kyiv, and are consolidating for a push to gain full control of the Donbas region of Eastern Ukraine. It's a messy war in the springtime slush and snow. Why?

The history of wars in Ukraine is (sort of) like the playing of a chess game. Queens invade and knights defend. Pawns are sacrificed and Bishops swoop like black ravens over the fields of the dead. Kings plot and mutter in their castles, while enemies besiege their walls. The great difference is that in *wars*, the victors take away with them parts of the chess board itself, and assemble their own patch-worked boards for others to challenge them on.

The world watches on anxiously. Is this the start of World War III? Why are the Russians fighting to gain control of Ukraine, and why are Ukrainians fighting to keep control? Nobody wants things taken from them by force, as any mugging victim can tell you. But what is the value of this small region to Russia?

The journalist's task is reporting events as they unfold. As I've gone along, though, I have become more and more captivated by that elusive "*why*" question. It's easy to photograph and describe a burned out tank that is still glowing hot—it's much harder to explain *why* it got here.

Once you ask the *why question*, you have to go digging for answers. Over the last 30 years or so, I have honed my investigative skills in both the present and the past. This book is my attempt to break into the vault of history and find the explanations that you need to understand why Vladimir Putin is *now* sending his ill-fated tanks to their fiery doom around Kyiv. I hope to weave a story, like the Bayeux Tapestry, but telling a narrative of a longer series of invasions and wars. If you follow me on this raid into the past, you will emerge with a heightened awareness of the dynamics of this little patch of land that armies have fought over across the millennia.

Pawn to king's fourth. Our game starts, strangely, with Viking longboats.

# PART 1. VIKINGS IN UKRAINE?

(Monticelli, 2020)

# Chapter 1. The Legacy of Kyivan Rus' ~650 CE

(Fazzeri, 2021)

*"The world of the Vikings was extensive. It stretched round the whole of Europe: from Scandinavia to the Mediterranean, along both easterly and westerly routes, and to the north-west to Iceland, Greenland and America. Throughout the Viking Age many sought their fortune in distant lands. Some remained there." –Else Roesdahl (The Vikings)*

The Vikings did not just raid the jeweled gold crosses and grain from fat abbeys in England. They also rowed their shallow-hulled pirate ships into the maze of European rivers, worming their way down the Dnieper River to the Black Sea. The pickings were thinner here, though, than in the European hinterland, with no cities or monasteries to conveniently amass treasure to make raids worthwhile. So, in the East, instead of taking treasure and going home, they took the land and stayed.

In this chapter, we'll watch the kingdoms of the Northmen rise and fall, up until the brink of the great communist commonwealth, and see what shadows of memory lie across the plains of Ukraine.

## The Origin of the Name "Rus"

I have occasionally gone looking for the original meaning of a name. The results vary in credibility. My name, "Marc" is said to variously derive from words meaning "warlike," "polite," "horse," or "virile!" The most credible sources seem to agree on a derivation from "Mars," and a meaning of "warlike."

The word "Russian" poses similar issues: Are they "the Red people" (which would fit the Norse—think of our term "rosy" and put it together with the frost-nipped face of a pale Norseman framed by a shock of ginger hair)? Or are they "The people who live on the Ros river" (Or is it called the Ros river because the Ros/Rus' established a base there)? Or does the name derive from the Finnish word "roets/ruotsi" which roughly means "rower" (Vasnetsov, 2019). Given the menace of the longboat emerging from the mist and reeds propelled by large warriors using long oars, I suspect this is the real origin of the word.

By about 750 CE, there were Scandinavian trading posts on the Dnieper River, close to the Black Sea in the Ukraine region, and Arab silver was making its way back to the Baltic nations, with Baltic furs traveling the other way. Those Scandinavian people were called "*The Rus*." It is not a small jump to see how that could become "*The Russians*" over time.

At around the same time, the enterprising Norsemen had also portaged their longboats into the great Volga River—on which four of Russia's great cities, including Moscow, were later to be established—and began to trade with the Arabs. The Islamic missionary, Ahmad ibn Fadlan, called these dangerous trading partners the "*Rusiya*." The name had stuck, and so have the Russians!

**Pirate Kingdom—the Kyivan State ~862**

The first great pirate city of Rus' was centered at the great trading hub of Kyiv. The Dnieper and Desna river systems flow into it, and it was a short portage way via the Desna River to the Volga. To the south lay the Black Sea; the back door to Constantinople with its fabled wealth. Constantinople—now Istanbul—was the capital city of the vast Eastern Christian empire (the Byzantine Empire). It dominated the Eastern Mediterranean until 1453, when the forces of Sultan Mehmed II besieged it and broke its resistance.

As the Scandinavian settlements around Ukraine became prosperous from the usual method of gaining and maintaining a stranglehold on trade routes, the Riurikid clan started to gain power. We must be a little skeptical about the main source of information on those early days, the so-called "Russian Primary Chronicle." This document appears to be some abbot's hobby historiography, and is described as "historical fiction"—but it's the earliest source we have, dating from about 1100. The story "Nestor the Chronicler'" tells is that Hroerek the Norseman was "invited" to be king of the Northwestern Russia Scandinavian settlements in 862. The "rule by invitation" theme has continued down the years, and has now become an important plank in Vladimir Putin's rationale for his dealings with Ukraine. The "voluntary" subjects of Hroerek became known as the "Riurik," and became a force to be reckoned with. They were reinforced by a stream of Swedish and Finnish mercenaries coming to seek their fortunes from the North—who meshed into a professional fighting class known as the Varangians. Hroerek died in about 879, and was succeeded by Helgi, who swept down and overran the prosperous city of the Jewish Khazars, Kyiv. Vikings will do what Vikings do.

This time, they realized that if they could keep control of the trade routes, they could get the silver without having to fight for it every time. Under Riurik rule, Kyiv became the center of a network of cities, each with its own king. One city emerged as dominant amongst the cities of the region—Kyiv. The kings of the lesser cities submitted to becoming princes in alliance with Kyiv, and gradually the princedoms merged into a unified state. By the end of the 900s, a combined "Kyivan Rus'" had become the major regional power.

### The Sudden Christianization of Kyivan Rus' 988

It was not easy being a Viking kingdom on land. The possibility of lightning raids followed by escape into the ocean mists was gone. If you took treasure by force, you also had to defend it by force. Vladimir "The Great," who ruled Kyivan Rus' from 980-1015 (after assassinating his brother for the throne), found it progressively harder to hold his kingdom together. The Bulgars, Slavic cousins of the Rus', were constantly harassing Vladimir's empire from the west, and proving remarkably resistant to conquest. The great Bulgar Empire with its Bulgarian Tsars had dominated the region between Ukraine and Constantinople. They were now in decline, but they were not an easy conquest. They fought back. Meanwhile, the lack of easy prosperity was fostering discontent in Vladimir's own ranks, including, ominously, his Varangian mercenaries from the fjords, who were showing signs of discontent.

Vladimir sent out ambassadors to assess whether forging an alliance with the Muslims, Christians, or Jews would best stabilize his empire. It is important to note that in those times, there was no such thing as a secular state. A nation state was *by definition* the army of some god or another. As an aside, it's fascinating to observe how much the most articulate secular state in the world, Russia, has reverted to using religion and religious symbolism in its 21st-century politics. Anyway, Vladimir's ambassadors reported that Constantinople seemed the best bet, with its strong walls, functional alliance network, and gleaming golden cupolas. It was strong and rich.

It was also very decidedly Christian, the Greek Orthodox Church having a major stake in the power structures of the Byzantine Empire. Vladimir reached out to Emperor Basil II in his capital city, Constantinople. Kyiv had nothing of the status and glory of Constantinople, but Basil II was having his own trouble with the Bulgars and bickering army chiefs. Vladimir caught Basil's attention by sacking Cherson, a stronghold of rebels against Basil, and offering 6000 hard-handed Varangian soldiers to help in Basil's wars. So, they worked out a deal. Vladimir would help Basil II with protecting his golden city. In return, he would marry Basil's sister Anna. As a codicil demanded by the church, Vladimir would also convert to Christianity, along with his people.

All the people of Kyivan Rus' got baptized in the Dnieper in a mass baptism. When the king tells you to become a Christian, you do it.

The Orthodox Church was very pleased at this sudden addition to their people power, adding weight to their cause in squabbling with Rome for control of the Mediterranean. Monks in the scriptorium wrote the history of their times; they thought Vladimir was Great.

## How Kyivan Rus' Got Fat—and Fell 1054-1242

Kyivan Rus' was where both Ukraine, and then Russia, began. Dictators create and use myths of history and the future, making it look like they have some sort of divine right and historical mandate to justify and glorify their territorial ambitions. To understand the current Ukrainian conflict, we have to explore how Putin looks at history and appeals to a certain viewpoint to give his actions the appearance of justice—what historians call his "historical mythology."

Kyivan Rus' prospered after the alliance with Constantinople. By the 1000s, the Empire covered an area from the White Sea in the north to the Black Sea in the south, and from Central Poland in the west to the eastern Crimean Peninsula. Slaves, honey, and furs flowed into southern markets, and silver and metalwork flowed the other way. Trade-route taxation fattened the Varangian warriors and slowly weakened their will to fight. From there, Kyivan Rus' slowly fragmented and faded until it was swallowed up entirely by Mongols in the mid-1200s, as they pressed westward with deadly force to expand their energetic new empire.

The Kyivan Rus' fortunes followed the usual rise-and-fall pattern of dynasties. The foundational stage was driven by enormous energy. Ad hoc solutions were put in place to control conquered people, and keep their newly acquired territories in sufficient peace, so as to not disrupt trade. For Kyivan Rus', that was the period from the first longboats to the reign of Vladimir the Great (~650-1015).

The second phase in a dynasty is the enrichment phase, often called its "golden age." For Kyivan Rus', that started with the Constantinople agreement of 988, followed by two centuries of unchallengeable power. Kyiv raked in huge profits, and prospered alongside Constantinople's dominance. The ruler of Constantinople had a standing army of Varangian bodyguards, exactly like the Swiss guard in the Vatican. Internal power struggles were still an issue for Kyivan Rus', however, and it was not until 1036 that Yaroslav "the Wise" gained total control. He produced a legal framework for his kingdom, the *Russkaya Pravda* (Russian Truth!), the first legal code for the Eastern Slavs, and the precursor of contemporary Russian law. By the end of the 1100s, the Norse had completely assimilated with the Slavs.

The decline and fall phase happens as the state becomes more concerned with tradition than expansion, and starts to breed inner competition. Yaroslav the Wise was a famous builder of churches, enhancing his prestige and control by co-opting the Church. He died in 1054, and was buried in one of the cathedrals he had built, St Sophia's. Then the princelings squabbled over the throne. Murder, war, and mayhem engulfed the state as province fought against province. At the same time, Constantinople's power was failing. The western Roman Catholic Church was launching repeated quasi-religious military expeditions—known as "crusades"—to try and wrest control of the Eastern Mediterranean from the Muslims. The crusades brought calamitous shifts in Mediterranean trade routes, and Constantinople lost its control of the movement of wealth.

In a series of decisive seasonal wars between 1237-1242, the Mongols broke the old Norse Empire, and that was the end of Ukrainian sovereignty for eight centuries.

## Northern Gods and Forgotten Graves—Society and Culture of Kyivan Rus'

The early Vikings colonizers took Slavic wives, who then raised the children of the Norse in the language and ways of the Slavs. A working father in those days would be absent for long periods on the longboats, and so the core culture (language and beliefs) would have been assimilated by the invaders within a couple of generations. The Kyivan Rus' morphed into a powerful Slavic tribe. They then became Christianized, and came under the influence of the Eastern Orthodox Church. Subsequently, they developed their own legal code. These were all milestones on a 700 year development of regional culture.

Culture consists of "symbols, language, beliefs, values, and artifacts" (PressBooks, 2010). The early culture of Kyivan Rus' makes for a fascinating study.

### *Language*

Both modern Russian and modern Ukrainian derive from the Ukrainian of the 10th century. Until about 700 years ago, Ukrainian *was* Russian, and Russian *was* Ukrainian. In 863, two missionaries were sent from Constantinople to oversee the newly "converted" people of the Ukraine. These brothers invented an alphabet that coped with the sounds of the Slavic dialect they chose for their first Bible translations, prompting the start of the written history of Ukraine. Unlike the western Church, which demanded that all its adherents speak and read Latin, the Orthodox Church invested heavily in translation into local languages, giving rise to early local-language literacy.

### *Beliefs, Values, Symbols, and Artifacts*

The early Ukranians had a warrior-culture through which they saw and understood their world.

The first religion of Ukraine was a loose coalition of Slavic, Finnic, and Norse pagan customs. Some physical traces of the early faith-ways of the Ukrainians are found in burial sites, and some scholars argue that the Russian Primary Chronicle contains coded references to ship burial, cremation in a burning house, funerary human sacrifices, and funeral feasting (Koptev, 2010). Sculptures of the gods Perun and Dubno have been unearthed, but not much is known of how they were worshiped. There are only a few hints in surviving rituals, like the famous decorated pysanky eggs of Ukraine.

Christian practices gradually syncretized with the old pagan rites, as the Orthodox Church labored to exert its control over the thinking and belief patterns of the newly "converted" nation. Kyivan Rus' became a key "Christian" player in the medieval "game of thrones."

The Kyivan Rus' culture idolized the effective fighter—the one who endured hardship and risked life in pursuit of conquest. The Russian Primary Chronicle breathes an admiration of the warrior's way. So, the Christianity of Kyivan Rus' was always inclined to praise and justify violence, without much appreciation of the irony of trying to match a crucified Jesus to the sword-wielding Varangian.

## The Golden Horde and Galicia-Volhynia 1237-1241

And then came the Mongols!

The Mongols were pushing out the boundaries of their central Asian empire in all directions. Led by the famous

Genghis Khan, the Mongol Empire began an ominous spread over Asia and Europe, and after his death, the Mongol army, the "Golden Horde," turned the empire into the largest ever border-to-border land empire in history.

From 1237-1241, the Golden Horde ransacked the palaces of the former ransackers. The fearsomely well equipped and well trained cavalry of Genghis Khan's grandson, Batu Khan, picked the golden fruit accumulated over centuries of dominance by Kyivan Rus'.

The Mongols completely upended the settled regimes of central Asia, and dominated Ukraine for 150 years. Ukraine survived as part of a vassal state, lumped together with Belarus in a region called Galicia-Volhynia, reduced to paying tribute to a Mongolian overlord.

### Key Takeaways

- The first recorded rulers of Ukraine came from Scandinavia.
- Ukraine's first political name was Kyivan Rus'.
- In 988, Kyivan Rus' was Christianized for political expediency.
- The Mongols conquered the Kyivan Rus'/Ukrainian empire in 1242.
- The old Norse culture was assimilated into a Christianized Slavic culture.

Ukraine is the birthplace of the Ukrainian and Russian people. For Russian readers of history, it raises the question: *If Russia started in Ukraine, why isn't it still part of Russia?* It is a territory that has been fought over since time immemorial, claimed and counterclaimed by invaders for millennia. Ukraine's boundaries have sometimes been determined by Ukrainians. Mostly, however, it has been given its shape by those who fought each other over it. For a Ukrainian, reading the history of the region provokes the question: *Do we belong to ourselves, or to some other world power*?

What happened to Ukraine next was uncounted generations of pain, as the once-great Viking nation fell into bondage under wave upon wave of aggressors.

# Chapter 2. Lithuanians, Poles, and Cossacks in Ukraine 1349-1795

(Muravitskiy, 2021)

*"In every age it has been the tyrant, the oppressor and the exploiter who has wrapped himself in the cloak of patriotism, or religion, or both to deceive and overawe the People." —Eugene Victor Debs* (Goodreads, 2022)

Ukrainians had to endure foreign rulers for centuries before they were again allowed the taste of freedom and self-determination. There are lessons here for every person who is living under outside control, or who has recently broken free.

The way the Polish and Lithuanians exploited Ukraine allows us to put the political forces of resistance and rebellion under the microscope. Parallels with the 2022 Russian invasion of Ukraine appear, and we are left to ask how a spirit of resistance and revolt can emerge from the wreckage of centuries of domination. Ukraine has figuratively faced the tanks before.

## Under Polish-Lithuanian Rule

Gradually, the western nations achieved military parity by learning from Mongol tactics and weaponry. In 1349, the Mongols lost their grip on Ukraine. Ukraine was not actually liberated, though, but assimilated (politically) by the Polish-Lithuanian empire.

Another power was rising in the west. After centuries of bloody battles against each other, Poland and Lithuania amalgamated to fight against everyone else (especially Hungary, at that point). In 1386, by a typically serpentine medieval set of dynastic inhertitances and marriages, Lithuania's Grand Duke Jogaila became both ruler of Lithuania and, simultaneously, the King of Poland. This dual-persona empire continued informally for almost 200 years, and their eventual "formal" treaty of union at Lublin in 1569 simply ratified the fact that they had become a juggernaut state with more than eight million people. Lublin had, ironically, once been a Kyivan Rus' stronghold. Under the logic of conquest, however, it had been reduced to just a small town in the mighty Polish-Lithuanian empire, and the memory of the Ukrainian state that it had once been part of was all but forgotten.

## Social and Economic Change, and Everything the Same

Territorial takeovers in medieval times meant the entire leadership of the subjected country simply transferred its allegiance to new rulers. In the case of Ukraine, the royalty was disbanded, but their lesser nobility kept its shape, with all its web of rank and subordination, down to the peasants and slaves. The entire nobility had to suck up a downgrade in status, though. A Kyivan Rus' lord was not as lordly as a Lithuanian lord.

For those at the bottom, nothing much changed, except that perhaps life got tougher. The Polish plowed up the fertile grasslands of Eastern Ukraine for bread and cake. In order to plant and harvest this new gold, peasants were invited to relocate, since peasant-power was hard to find in the Ukrainian steppes. The government incentivized them by offering freedom from serfhood (the system where certain laborers belonged to certain estates and were not allowed to move). That sparked a people-movement of peasants who were longing for more freedom. When they arrived in the wheatlands, living conditions were much improved. The great Ukrainian estates thrived under their Polish landlords, and grain flowed westward.

## Religion and Culture

The Ukrainian peasants were staunchly Eastern Orthodox. It became expedient to their nobles, however, to convert to western, Latin Catholicism. Roman Catholic monasteries, churches, and schools began to creep into Ukraine. The lease-holders of the great estates were largely Jewish. This was a socio-economic-religious mix which had much the same properties as charcoal-potassium nitrate-sulfur; a spark could cause a severe reaction.

## The Formative Phase

All was tranquil, however, in the embrace of Poland. Nobility sought to "Polify" themselves as quickly as possible. The mercantile cities recovered, and centers like Kyiv still had an enviable situation on the trade routes. A merchant-class began to increase in the cities, as traders earned enough to buy security and status. The aspirations of the poor were partially addressed by work as freemen on the wheatfields. The Ukrainians settled down, for the most part, in their role as a colonized people.

The Polish-Lithuanian Commonwealth sensibly allowed everyone freedom of religion, an important policy for a state that included so much diversity. Historically, invaders of Ukraine had taken three approaches to Eastern Orthodoxy in their conquered territory. One approach was to try and forcibly place all adherents under a more biddable authority in Rome or Moscow. The second, favored by the communists, was to try and destroy the power of the Church altogether. And the third approach, which the Polish-Lithuanian empire took, was to make it worth the while of the Church to toe the line, and keep its adherents in check. Local Christians could do all the religious things they wanted to, in their own way, but the hierarchy of the Church knew that they were also responsible for keeping their members from revolting against the regime.

In the dying days of the Polish Peace, in 1580, Ostroh (West of Kyiv) became a major center of learning. Ostroh had a new-fangled printing press, and produced the first ever whole Bible in Slavonic. The first printing of the Bible in a local language has often been a step toward educating the poor, implanting rebellious thoughts of the equal worth of all humans, and supporting rebellious actions (Sanneh, 2009).

The Ukrainians had a need for guidance into rebellion. Things were about to get very much worse for the descendants of the Northmen.

## The Great Revolt and the Rule of the Cossacks 1648

The plots and plans of the Roman Church brought an end to this fragile Polish equilibrium. The metropolitan (archbishop) of Kyiv and most of his clergy signed a unity agreement with Rome. The 1596 Synod of Brest transferred all the Kyivan Orthodox believers, under their priests, *en masse* into the Catholic Church. This "Uniate" Church could govern itself, still have married clergy, and still conduct its worship in proto-Russian Slavonian. It caused great tensions.

Meanwhile, in the badlands of the wild south of Ukraine, a new political force was emerging: The Cossacks. Their name emerged from the Turkish "kazak," which meant "free man" (think about Kazakhstan!). They started off as a loose coalition of hunters and honey-gatherers, but under external pressure they had banded together into a pirate kingdom, much like the early Rus'. By the mid-1500s, they had become a famous fighting force, with a determinedly egalitarian philosophy of leadership. You led if you could, and you led if others let you lead. This was especially appealing to Ukrainian serfs. Once an oversupply of labor developed in the wheatlands, the landlords reimposed serfdom, which triggered a major migration of serfs to the land of the Cossacks.

At first, the Polish overlords enjoyed being able to hire the Cossacks as mercenaries to settle border wars with the savage peoples further east (including the Muscovites). In peacetime, however, they were difficult to control. They were adept at using either horses or boats, and could not be subdued by conventional marching-army tactics.

The Cossacks buzzed and stung along the southern and eastern flanks of the Commonwealth, growing in number, expertise, and power. Ideologically, they identified themselves as Eastern Orthodox, making a welcome home for disaffected Ukrainians. They skirmished their way deeper and deeper into the heartland of Ukraine. In 1620, the entire garrison of Kyiv decided to reconvert to Eastern Orthodoxy, and with the threat of the Orthodox Cossacks knocking on the doors, they re-established Orthodoxy as the official religion of the region. Let the battle over who owned which church building begin!

The Orthodox Church flourished, and Ukraine enjoyed a brief cultural revival. Petro Mohyla (the new Orthodox Metropolitan) led with energy and restored public respect for Ukrainian culture. It became possible for Ukrainian learning to thrive, and Ukraine's first university was established, the Kyivan Mohyla Academy.

The respite was only very brief for Ukraine, however. In 1648, everyone began killing each other again.

The leader of the revolt was a Cossack officer named Khmelnytsky, who had fled Ukraine for Cossack-held territories, and was elected *Hetman* (meaning "headman," unsurprisingly!) He started mobilizing an invasion force and coordinating local rebellions all over Ukraine. Liberation was in the air!

Kyivan rulers sent for a Polish army to put down the rebellion, but in May 1648, Khmelnytsky defeated them in two well-judged battles. Ukrainian peasants revolted and killed Polish landlords, Latin priests, and Jewish financiers. Khmelnytsky won another decisive battle against the Poles, launched a lightning raid into Poland itself, and returned to Kyiv as liberator.

Freedom, however, was to come with a distinctly Cossacky flavor.

Khmelnytsky set up Ukraine as a Cossack state, with Cossack officers taking over the role of the ousted Polish gentry. The peasants began to roll their eyes. Poland continued to press from the west, and the Tatars were still sniping on the east. Then, despite all his initial liberationist popularity, Khmelnytsky opened the door for the next great repression of Ukraine—he invited the Muscovites to help him in his wars. Ukraine concluded a treaty with Russia at Pereiaslav in 1654.

**The Ruin 1654–1687**

The Russian Tsar accepted the invitation with glee. It was exactly the opportunity he needed to consolidate and expand his western borders. Russian school history textbooks say that the Ukrainians accepted the sovereignty of the Tsar in exchange for protection. *Ukrainian* school history textbooks, in contrast, say that instead of helping Ukraine achieve sovereignty, the Tsar reneged on his word and subjected Ukraine to Russian rule.

His troops swept into the area—and stayed. Khmelnytsky died. Ukraine was filled with fighting between the Cossack officers (who rapidly became their own hereditary ruling class). Poland and Russia faced off over Ukrainian territories. Then the Turks of the Ottoman Empire suddenly emerged as players from the south. Soon, there was nothing left of Ukraine worth invading, except its rich black soil. It is a period that is known in Ukrainian history books simply as "The Ruin."

Out-manouvered by the machinations of the powerful, Ukrainians' last hope of self-determinacy lay with the remnants of the Hetmanate. Cossack leaders were the most likely to care about the land itself.

## The Hetmanate

From 1663, Ukraine was roughly divided down the middle along the Dnieper River—the western half (confusingly called the Right Bank), and the eastern half (the so-called Left Bank, rowing downstream). Poland dominated the Right, and Russia the Left. The two sides installed their own compliant Hetmans (always Cossacks), and the Ukrainians were allowed to till their soil and milk their cows on behalf of others, as before.

In 1686, the Russians and Poles formalized the situation with the "Treaty of Eternal Peace." Everything changed as alliances shifted. Poland and Russia became allies (because of Sweden, but that's another story!), but Poland felt as though it had been taken advantage of, and the situation on the ground in Polish-occupied Ukraine became volatile. Left Bank Ukraine invaded Right Bank Ukraine in 1672 in search of unity and independence, backed by the Ottoman Turks. Unsurprisingly, that resulted in *Turkish* control and exploitation for a quarter of a century, until Poland regained control in 1699. The next year, the Polish dissolved the Right Bank Hetmanate, opting for more reliable direct rule from Warsaw.

The Left Bank Hetmanate limped on with a flimsy illusion of Ukrainian autonomy. Tsar Peter I of Russia had summarily appropriated the "Russian" identity for his growing empire in 1721, by renaming his empire "The *Russian* Empire." He did *not* consult the Ukrainians, the descendants of the Kyivan Rus'. The Tsar hand picked his own Hetman for Ukraine, and culturally, the architecture, music, and dance abandoned Poland and turned toward Moscow for inspiration.

Eventually, however, Ivan Mazepa, a Hetman picked by Tsar Peter I, tried to wage a war of independence against Russia (Sweden was involved again). The Russians crushed the revolution brutally and imposed complete control over the Hetmancy, reducing it to a mere ceremonial office, with no independent authority at all. Eventually, Catherine the Great, Russia's longest-reigning empress, did away with the vestiges of the Hetmancy altogether, in 1764.

The merchants of the middle class survived and prospered on the chaos, as it often does—armies need supplies of food and arms, and traders continue to control such commodities. War always has its economic opportunities, after all. The merchants were an important anchor stopping the ship of state drifting into war too easily, or too far. Wars are fought to advance or secure prosperity, and it is the merchants who handle the flow of money and goods.

## The Disappearance of Poland-Lithuania

Strangely enough, some features of democracy were adopted by the Polish-Lithuanian Commonwealth, and played out to some extent in Ukraine. There was an odd concern that monarchs might need to be controlled. Of course, the *peasants* were not allowed to vote, but nobles voting for a non-hereditary king was a step in the democratic direction. In 1791, the Commonwealth even adopted a constitution, the second in the world after the USA. Under the influence of the French Revolution and the American Revolutionary War, the acceptability of raw conquest began to be questioned by some intellectuals.

Sadly, none of this had time to trickle down to the Ukranians. The Poland-Lithuanian Commonwealth was rapidly imploding. By 1795, the Austrians, Prussians, and Russians had divided it into bits by treaty, and taken possession. When the new edition of the map of Europe appeared, there was no more Poland or Lithuania. Russia had already annexed Crimea from the Mongols in 1783 (does this ring any bells?). Most of the rest of Ukraine, the so-called "Right Bank" and the former Polish province of

Volhynia (inhabited mostly by Ukrainians), slipped into Russian hands.

**Key Takeaways**

- In 1349, Poland defeated the Mongols and assumed possession of Ukraine.
- Poland exerted linguistic, economic, and religious influence on Ukraine.
- The Polish-Lithuanian Commonwealth allowed freedom of religion for Ukrainians.
- In 1648, the Cossacks beat back the Polish, and took over control of Ukraine.
- Russia took control of Eastern Ukraine from the Cossacks in 1654.
- The Russians and Polish divided Ukraine between themselves in 1686.
- In 1721, Tsar Peter I named his empire "Russia," including his territory in Ukraine.
- In 1795, the Austrians and Prussians took over Western Ukraine from Poland-Lithuania.

Ukranians are desperate to preserve their freedom, because it was so recently won, whereas Russians are desperate to regain control over Ukraine, because it has so recently lost it. Power alignments were often forced upon Ukraine. But in the midst of the carnage, democratic and egalitarian impulses began to find expression, giving Ukraine some hope in its quest for autonomy.

The Polish-Lithuanian Commonwealth lasted for about 400 years (1386-1795). The Russian state—from Ivan the Terrible until today—has lasted for 475 years (1547-2022). As major players go on the volatile Eurasian scene, it's overdue for a major down-scaling in influence. Next up, we take a closer look at Russia's crucial middle centuries, and how they affected Ukraine as we know it today.

# Chapter 3. Ukraine Under Imperial Rule

## 1795-1917

(Vorobyev, 2017)

*"I shall never, under any circumstances, agree to a representative form of government because I consider it harmful to the people whom God has entrusted to my care." —Tsar Nicholas II* (Alpha History, 2022)

Our investigations bring us to the Old Bear himself, the Tsar of Russia.

The Russian *myth* of willing submission was not able to actually *achieve* willing submission. The history of Imperial Russia's rule over Ukraine is one of grudging subservience and official propaganda, with Ukrainians always on the lookout for safe places to keep the flame of nationalism alive.

## Two Eagles, Four Heads—Two Empires in Ukraine

Both Russia and Austria had double-headed eagles in their coat of arms. The hungry eagles agreed to *share* Ukraine—but they both wanted it all.

If the land in Ukraine is not being strafed with tank fire or seeded with landmines, it has the potential to feed millions. It also stands squarely between Russia or Austria and the Black Sea, causing profit-reducing tolls to be levied on goods entering and leaving. If a nation were to *own* Ukraine, then there would be no hindrance to the prosperity of the nation that had possession.

The reason for wanting to own Ukraine was simple and obvious; the only problem was taking it and making it stick. Russia and Austria had each gotten part-way to their goal. Now they were eyeing each other.

### *Ukraine Under the Austrian Empire*

Austria emerged from the collapse of Poland-Lithuania in possession of a scrap of Ukrainian territory, the province of Galicia. Maria Theresa and Joseph II, who ruled Austria together as mother-and-son empress and emperor from 1765-1780, opted for the "make the oppressed happy" approach. They limited the amount of money they tried to squeeze out of the peasants, and outlawed the virtual slavery to landlords. As the 1780s rolled on, the cities revived as trade flowed again. Ukrainians were granted more rights and privileges. Education in Ukrainian (rather than Latin or Russian) was permitted in primary schools.

Ukrainian territories under Austrian rule answered to Vienna. Although Ukrainians were not permitted any political self-determination, the more *laissez-faire* approach of the Austrian Empire fostered the growth of Ukrainian national consciousness.

## *The Stirrings of Ukrainian National Consciousness*

### *1848*

As long as the Ukrainians ate Ukrainian food (beetroot borscht, paska, and varenyky) and spoke Ukrainian, they would remain Ukrainian. In Western Ukraine, national consciousness began to revive as the strength of Austria began to weaken, especially after the civil unrest that swept the Austrian Empire around 1848. The Ukrainians started organizing small local militias, and pushing for secession. The first Ukrainian-language newspaper began to circulate. The tax on peasants was eventually abolished in 1848.

## *Crimean War and the Emancipation of Ukrainian Serfs 1856*

Meanwhile, in the parts of the Ukrainian territory that it controlled, Russia adopted a different "reform" process to deal with the perceived threat of Ukrainian nationalism. In 1839, the Uniate Church was dissolved and incorporated in the Russian Orthodox matrix. The Orthodoxy of Ukraine was now completely "russified"–Ukrainians were all Orthodox, but had to answer to the Metropolitan of Moscow, not Kyiv.

Ukraine under Russian control had far less freedom of identity than Ukraine had under Austrian rule. Russia strictly censored the press and curtailed civil freedoms, constantly pushing the *we are all Russians* policy. Cossack officers were russified by giving them the same status as Russian nobles. Under Catherine II, the peasants were forced into the "corvée" system, where they had to work for a landlord in lieu of rent.

That serfdom lasted until after Russia's defeat in the Crimean War in 1856, although they were only fully emancipated five years later, in 1861. However, they still had to perform all the rural labor functions they had performed before. History teaches that political elites exact benefits from the discounted labor of the poor, as well as cash benefits from taxing them. The Poles, Cossacks, Austrians, and Russian Tsars (and later the Russian Communist Party) all had different political dispensations—but in each of them, the Ukrainian peasants played the same role. Ukraine continued to be a nation of peasants under foreign rule.

## Socioeconomic Change

Life under Austrian control continued to be hard for the peasants. The population began to increase, but there was no industry to give workers a livelihood. A massive exodus of young workers to the Americas began to gain momentum in the late 1800s.

In Russian-controlled Ukraine, mining operations started to draw workers to the mines and new industries. Local Ukrainian excess labor preferred to move on to other agricultural opportunities—if not in Ukraine, then further afield in the Americas. The city of Odessa blossomed as a Russian-controlled trading center on the Black Sea. These new Russian workers were the seedbed of the Russian population of Eastern Ukraine today.

The components of 21st-century Ukraine were beginning to come together.

## Don't Educate the Peasants! Intelligentsia and Ukrainian Activism

Peasants, unexpectedly, turned out to be able to exert formidable pressure on governments if they could be organized, which next happened under the leadership of those "illiterate peasants" who managed to get degrees.

Kharkiv University, founded in 1805, became the bastion of Ukrainian cultural resistance. It produced Ukrainian scholarship, and was a center for publishing in Ukrainian and for the international academic community. Two other "Ukrainian" universities were set up in Kyiv (1834) and Odessa (1865). They were sponsored by Russia, but they could legitimately focus on Ukrainian culture and history. Literature on all things Ukrainian became available in the Ukrainian language, and was eagerly consumed by an increasingly knowledgeable and nationalistic audience.

These books stimulated a burgeoning self-awareness amongst Ukranians in the 1800s. Taras Shevchenko was one key author. A group of Ukrainian artists had bought him out of serf-bondage as a child, as he showed so much promise in drawing. Although he indeed became an important painter, his most influential role was as a poet. His poetry has the flavor of William Blake—surreal and rural, epic and fantastic, religious and excoriatingly "prophetic" (political). He was the poet of a free Ukraine; a visionary whose powerful Ukrainian verse entered the soul of the subjugated, and put fire in the belly of revolutionaries.

This did not sit well with the authorities. A new ban on Ukrainian literature was imposed. At every level of education, Russian language instruction was reintroduced and enforced. The Russians arrested Shevchenko and exiled him to the Ural Mountains, where he instantly became a martyr to the cause of Ukrainian self-determination. His work circulated illicitly, and banning his work made it all the more treasured among true Ukrainian patriots. Unsurprisingly, Ukrainian language and poetry thrived underground.

Austrian-controlled Ukraine then became the center of Ukrainian publishing, with proscribed literature smuggled back to secret readers in the east. Galicia, the former Polish province with its large Ukrainian population, became the main supporter of insurrection in Russian-occupied Ukraine.

## Eastern Galicia: A Bastion of Ukrainianism

Ukrainians began to organize themselves politically. The Cyril and Methodius Brotherhood (a secret society) operated from Austrian-controlled Galicia. Founded in 1845, it promoted social equality, and held a vision for a "United Slavic States," drawing all the Slavic Nations in the region into a commonwealth (led by the Ukrainians, of course). Somebody betrayed their secret, though, and they were savagely exterminated in 1847.

Tsarist suppression was never able to meld the unwilling Ukrainians into a greater Russia. From the 1850s onwards, independent secret societies called *hromadas* started to spring up all over the place. Because they were not centrally controlled, they were impossible to wipe out. Student-led *hromadas* soon took a more openly radical stance, and eventually one Kharkiv *hromada* formed itself into the Revolutionary Ukrainian Party. Its motto in 1900 was "one, single, indivisible, free, independent Ukraine" (Encyclopedia Britannica, 2022).

The Russian revolution of 1905 did impact Ukraine, but it was an essentially internal Russian struggle of communists against Tsarists. Ukrainians might have been agitating for freedom, but independence for Ukraine was never on the agenda of a communist movement that aimed at world-wide imposition of its vision of society.

The children of those early Vikings had nowhere to go. They could not row back up the Dnieper and find refuge in the Northern fjords; that ship had sailed. Ukrainians had to stand their ground, marshall their forces, and bide their time.

### Key Takeaways

- Austria granted limited cultural and religious freedoms to Ukrainians under their rule, but forced Ukrainians to labor as serfs.
- In areas of Ukraine ruled by Russia, Russia suppressed uniquely Ukrainian expression of culture, and attempted to make Ukrainians Russian.
- Ukraine continued to provide minerals and food to Austria and Russia.
- Ukrainian nationalism flourished underground, under the leadership of a growing core of Ukrainian intellectuals.
- By the 1850s, Ukrainians began to organize themselves politically through secret societies.

In political situations like Ukraine, one party considers the other to be dissidents unjustifiably fostering division. Meanwhile, the other party considers the first lot to be oppressors brutally thwarting the legitimate aspirations of a captive nation. Point of view is key, therefore, in evaluating claims and counter-claims with regard to Ukraine. Mother-tongue education always becomes a rallying point for controlled nations' aspirations against controlling nations.

Tertiary education gives revolutionaries skills in research, communication, and leadership that facilitates seperatist movements, and young students are more inclined to spearhead political revolt because of their youthful recklessness and idealism. Russia and Ukraine have each had their own interpretation of history for a very long time, and this contestation for "true" history is the ideological motor for governance.

As we next look into the two revolutions—the great Russian revolt and the simultaneous little Ukrainian revolt—we will observe how the sociology of revolution does not differ much from the sociology of conservative rulers. Power belongs to those who can wield it the most efficiently.

# PART 2. UKRAINE IN THE 20th CENTURY

(Pylypenko, 2019)

# Chapter 4. The Start of the 20th Century for Ukraine 1900-1922

(British Library, 2019)

*"Strength does not come from winning. Your struggles develop your strengths." —Arnold Schwarzenegger*

Ukraine entered the 20th century as a mere shadow of its swashbuckling 9thcentury glory. The world population had become too big, and there were no more empty or lightly guarded lands; no more river systems to slip away into. If you could not stand and fight, you had to endure exploitation or extermination. You had to bide your time and nurse your strength, and wait for a leader who could lead you against your oppressor.

Ukraine had fallen very low. We will now take stock of what options remained for the shattered remnants of Kyivan Rus'.

## The Power of Culture: How Ukraine Survived

If a large enough population maintains enough of its culture, it always has the potential to regroup. At the beginning of the 20th century, there were 25 million Ukranians—a very significant number in a total world population of only 2 billion. Ukrainian culture proved very resistant to eradication or assimilation.

### *Language*

The Ukrainian and Russian languages share about 60% of their vocabulary (Bermel, 2022), with fewer similarities than between Italian and Portuguese. They have diverged from each other into two distinct languages, with Ukrainian absorbing Polish and Austrian influences.

The Russians had systematically made *sure* that Ukrainian did not develop into a language for intellectuals. The banning of Ukrainian as a language of instruction in schools had put the language under extreme pressure. However, under the shadow of Russia, the language of Ukraine became a core component of Ukrainian resistance and aspirations. The Russians repeatedly tried to ban all Ukrainian books and newspapers—a policy that always failed. Also, restricting the language of education to Russian did not have the desired Russification effect, partly because they had previously "peasantified" the bulk of the population by limiting their access to education. No school meant no Russian. The unforeseen consequence was that the two policies worked together to keep Ukrainians away from Russian influence.

## *Religion*

The philosopher Karl Marx, the great exponent of the socio-economic communist vision, might have warned against religion as "flowers on the chains of the proletariat" (Marx, 1843), but both the Russian Tsars and the Communist Party that followed them made sure that Russians were holding the end of the Ukrainians' chain-of-religion. Russians were mockingly atheist in their rhetoric. Pragmatically, however, the Russians knew that if the *state* could control the religion of the masses, you could have power over its adherents. The transfer of the Ukrainian Church to the "pastoral oversight" of the metropolitan of Moscow in the middle of the 19th century had been a straightforward play for control of the Ukrainian soul.

A politically conscious national church network, functioning in the language of the subjugated, provides a focal-point for national resistance. If every cupola on every little church in every little village is a proclamation of God's delight in a *Ukrainian* congregation, that would be a major boost to nationalist aspirations. The Russians understood that, and they thought they had eliminated the threat. Adherence dropped to a low point of 39% in 1991.

All was not as it seemed, however. The Ukrainian Orthodox Church might be in eclipse, but it had hidden reserves of strength, as it waited for the right circumstances to roar back into life.

### *Education*

At the turn of the 20th century, there were only three universities for Ukrainians, at Kyiv, Lviv, and Chernivsti. If you were Cossack or Russian, they were open to all. If you were Jewish or Ukrainian or Polish, you would be allowed to apply, subject to quotas. They were, nonetheless, places where some clever Ukrainian peasants could receive the gift of time to reflect, and the philosophical tools to *think*. Thinking is one of the things oppressive regimes cannot afford to allow people to do.

The language of the universities was overwhelmingly Russian or Polish. In 1906, most courses at Lviv University were given in Russian. There were 185 Polish courses, 19 in Ukrainian, 14 in Latin, and 5 in German (Canadian Institute of Ukrainian Studies, 2001). You had to be a polyglot to survive at a university in your own country.

As a result of such obstacles, there were extremely few educated Ukrainians. Even a *few* intellectuals, however, can influence a great many leaders who filtered back into Ukrainian society with ideas of national self-determination and respect for one's culture. Ukrainian teachers were a formidable force. Like the Church, an educated cadre was a chess piece carefully positioned. Its value would become apparent as the game progressed.

### *Overseas Populations*

One of Ukraine's cultural resources over the years were the overseas populations of Ukranians. Half a million Ukrainians had emigrated to the Americas before WWI. Most of those went into mining and industry in the US, but about 100,000 found a new home in Canada. These sympathizers were useful to Ukraine's rising nationalism. They provided a haven for refugees, funds to support the resistance, and, most of all, a platform for free speech. The oldest Ukrainian newspaper in the States is *Svoboda* ("liberty"), which was first published in New Jersey in 1893. Illicit copies regularly found their way back to Ukraine.

Having a large, vocal population of overseas advocates was important. It gets harder to manipulate events and records if the world press shows an interest in what you are doing. Ukraine was gradually putting pieces of its own into play in the war-games over Ukraine.

### *Economics*

Funding was an issue for Ukrainian independence, because Ukrainians had been deliberately impoverished. Russia controlled the food production and mining and industry of Ukraine, and everything was railed northwards to Moscow for notional "redistribution." It proved costly in every way to struggle for national independence. At the start of the 1900s, Ukrainians could afford very little resistance. State funding was available for things like Russian education and monumental statuary, but never for support of Ukrainian culture.

### *Revolutionary Organization*

Russia, on the other hand, had many resources to pour into intelligence gathering and suppression of resistance. Around 1900, Ukraine had only a vestigial resistance network. Coordination of concerned Ukrainians was especially difficult, since 80% of Ukrainians lived in the countryside. Mobilization of armed groups is a city-activity, where the logistics of recruitment, weapon supply, and cover are facilitated by crowded conditions. In the cities, however, the secret police were king of the shadows.

Marxist theory was circulating like wildfire in the Russia and Ukraine of the 1900s. Marx's idea was that if the conditions for the workers became bad enough, they would inevitably rise in coordinated revolt, and replace their oppressors with more acceptable leadership. In Ukraine, it seemed that communism was a magic key to opening the door of independence—all of Marx's factors for inevitable revolution were in place: An oppressed proletariat, an oppressive foreign bourgeoisie, and revolutionary cells in place.

## Brewing Revolution: Russian Communists and Ukrainian Peasants Raise the Stakes

Russia had been growing in Eurasian regional influence for 50 years, and the surrounding nations had fought to limit its power. Napoleon Bonaparte of France targeted Russia, intending to make it join in his blockade of Britain. However, his ill-fated winter raid of 1812 was repulsed by the weather, as well as hard-bitten Russian resistance. Then the Russians lost against the French, Turks, and British in Crimea. This war between Russia and her neighbors played itself out on Ukrainian territory. Ukraine was wary of war, and the credibility of the Tsars was at an all time low. Peasant rebellions became a permanent feature of the Russian landscape, each time savagely ridden down by the empire's cavalry. The state instituted some cosmetic reforms, but the Tsar grimly held onto his royal prerogatives.

Ukraine contributed vigorously to the unrest that brought down the Tsars. Workers took strike action. Peasants rioted and burned. In return, Tsarist soldiers slaughtered civilians. The Ukrainian dream of "rule by the Ukrainian proletariat" was ardently promoted in secret.

One of Russia's unsatisfactory reforms at that time was the institution of *dumas*, or parliaments, where different regions could send delegates to represent regional interests. In the first and second *dumas*, the Ukrainian delegates formed a caucus to push Ukrainian concerns. The Tsar changed the *duma* rules after that, specifically to break the power of special interest blocs. He decreed that all delegates had to speak with a single voice, and not refer to the issues shared by several delegates and the states they represented. With their powers of expression so severely curtailed, all that made its way through the hot air of the *dumas* was that Russia should *think about letting Ukrainians speak*

*Ukrainian*, and *have a little more autonomy*. It was a waste of time.

## Ukraine, Russian Revolution, and Hungary 1917

Then came the incomprehensible idiocy of the First World War. Ukraine was drawn into the conflict because Imperial Russia was on the side of France and Britain against Austria-Hungary and Germany. They had no option to remain neutral. War rolled over them again.

Western Ukraine became a battlefront between Russian forces fighting against Austrians and Hungarians. Many Ukrainians were shot as suspected "Russian sympathizers" by the Austrians, as the Red Army pushed Austria back westwards over Ukraine in 1916. The Red Army continued on into Austrian territory and took ethnically Ukrainian Galicia-Volhynia. Ironically, the Russians also considered the Ukrainians dangerous, and immediately shot many suspected "*Austrian* sympathizers." Then, ludicrously and tragically, the next year the German coalition punched back and reconquered all the territory Russian had gained. As they say in Africa, *when the elephants fight, the grass is trampled.*

Fueled by the bright hope of a communist utopia (we'll all share everything), the intelligentsia-led proletariat shook the thrones of the mighty, and wrenched the course of world history sideways. The Bolsheviks staged their 1917 Red October Revolution. The Tsarist Regime abruptly collapsed. The chaotic political aftermath was "won" by the communist Bolsheviks ("bolshevik" means "majority." They mysteriously spun a minority into a majority).

Ukraine followed the Bolsheviks' lead and declared themselves the Ukrainian People's Republic, with Kyiv as capital. The Central Council (Rada) espoused socialism as the governing theory for the new republic.

## Brief Independence for Ukraine 1918-1922

It was to be an all-too-brief respite for Ukraine, though. The Great War reached its Armistice, but the lesser war for Ukraine waged on. The *Rada* lasted for a year, followed by another Hetmanate for a few months, followed by three months of the Ukrainian National Council of the West Ukrainian People's Republic, followed finally by the Directorate of the Ukrainian People's Republic from November 1918 to 1922.

The *Rada's* mandate was autonomous statehood, but pro-Russian workers' and soldiers' coalitions opposed it bitterly. There had been no discussion in communist circles on what might happen if revolutionary leaders turned out to be as exploitative as the old lot. The Bolshevics considered that they themselves were by definition the "revolutionary party." Ukrainian nationalism, therefore, was deemed "counter-revolutionary," something that should be stamped out.

Communist parties quickly and efficiently dominated Russia's surrounding states with populist rhetoric and Russian backup. In 1922, under intense pressure from

Russia, Belarus, Transcaucasia, Russia and Ukraine formed the core of the USSR. This newly formed "united states of central Asia" formed a single country, with almost the same boundaries as the toppled Tsarist Empire. Ukraine had gone through a bloody revolution, only to end up where it had been before—a subjugated vassal state.

In the far Western Ukrainian-dominant areas that were outside the original Ukrainian Soviet State, Hungary had taken control of the region of Transcarpathia. The main political contest there was whether you leaned toward Budapest or Moscow. Ukrainian aspirations were ignored, and took many years to emerge as a political force. Ukrainians, everywhere, were under house arrest.

**Key Takeaways**

- Ukrainian culture has kept Ukraine from being swallowed up by any of the nations that have controlled her.
- Language, religion, and education are critical systems that have maintained Ukrainian self-identity.
- Large overseas Ukrainian communities have also fostered Ukrainian nationalism and the fight for self-determination.
- Ukraine fought against the Tsars alongside the communists.
- From 1918-1922, Ukraine was an independent nation.
- In 1922, Ukraine was compelled into solidarity and functional vassalship with Russia in the USSR.

Cultural cohesion enables subjected nations like Ukraine to remain as cohesive units despite being subjugated by more powerful nations. Meanwhile a growing consensus was emerging that nations ought to be answerable to the opinion of a global community of nations.

Ukraine had a few brief years of independence, but was still too weak to maintain its grip on self-determination. Next up, we shall consider what life under the Russian-led USSR was like for Ukrainians, and how they developed their capacity to take their chance at independence, when it eventually arrived.

# Chapter 5. Lenin, Stalin, and WWII 1922-1953

(Skitterphoto, 2017)

*"Attention must be devoted principally to raising the workers to the level of revolutionaries; it is not at all our task to descend to the level of the "working masses." – Vladimir Lenin, 1901* (Vladimir Ilyich Lenin Internet Archives, 2022)

The name "Vladimir" means "The glory of princes," highly ironic for leaders in a movement devoted to the abolition of the bourgeoisie/ruling classes. Russian babies, though, have been named after the great Kyivan Rus' prince, ever since Vladimir of Kyiv converted to Christianity in 987 CE. It is a very common name; and it has been carried by some formidable "princes" of Communist Russia—Vladimir Ilyich Lenin, for one. Lenin was head of Soviet Russia from the 1917 revolution until his death in 1924, as well as head of the Union of Soviet Socialist Republics (USSR) from 1922 until his death. The man had serious power at his command.

Ukrainians have cause to remember Vladimir Lenin. The memories are very dark. We must traverse those terrible days in this chapter.

## Vladimir Lenin and Ukraine

Ukraine resisted Russian rule with a passion Lenin had not expected.

Lenin's gambit, similar to developments in Ukraine in 2022, was to promote and arm a pro-Russian rival, in the form of the Bolshevik Ukrainian State in the east of the country. This was made plausible by the many ethnically Russian workers in mining and industry there. They went to war against the Kyiv regime, but were at first beaten by unexpectedly passionate resistance. Even Bolshevik-sympathizing Ukrainians were so culturally nationalistic that it was hard to motivate them to fight against Kyiv.

Russia, however, continued to support pro-Bolshevik Ukrainian forces, which put the Kyiv-based government under pressure on many fronts. Going back to the end of WWI, the Russians signed a side-deal with Poland which then suddenly owned chunks of Western Ukraine. Then Lenin struck his decisive deal—Russia offered Ukraine self-government "equal to that of Russia," if Ukraine agreed to co-found the Union of Soviet Socialist Republics. The package included a secure territory of its own and a mode of government, language of choice, and systems of education and religion of its own choice. It was an attractive bait.

## The USSR Harvest of Ukrainian Wheat

The politics of food has always preoccupied great nations. Lenin desperately wanted a settled Ukraine because of Russian food security. Starvation in Russia during 1918 almost collapsed the Bolsheviks. If Moscow were to have the first option on Ukrainian wheat, it would solve that problem. In addition, Bolshevik theory denied the reality of individual nations, which justified raids from Russia into Ukraine to establish collectivized wheat farms. In 1920, the Ukrainian wheatlands fell into the hands of Russian-led collectivists. The loss of control over Ukrainian wheat was another pressure pushing Ukraine into the USSR.

With the formation of the USSR, Russian free access to Ukrainian resources was guaranteed. Ukrainian wheat farming revived somewhat, harvests started rolling in, and rolling stock started to take tons of wheat northwards to the bakeries of Moscow. Revolutionary freedom for Ukraine meant that only the *direction* of the traffic in wheat had changed. *Polish* wheat simply became *Russian* wheat.

## The Ukrainization of Ukraine?

In Ukraine, the peasants were revolting against the Revolutionary Party. This ambivalence has run through all communist dealings with Ukraine. Ukrainians had been united by the dream of independence. Lenin set out to subvert such inclinations with all the craft and power at his disposal. If Moscow *had* to eat Ukrainian bread, Ukrainians must be *made* to *want* to send it.

Lenin's first essay in appeasing the Ukrainians was a push in the 1920s for Russia to make everything look more Ukrainian—*korenizatsiya*, they called it, "getting back to our roots." The propaganda push involved promoting Ukrainian language, and sponsoring Ukrainian cultural institutions in education and religion. It did not produce the desired effect, so pacification by cultural friendliness gave way to far worse measures, orchestrated by the extraordinarily ruthless Joseph Stalin.

## Stalin's Pacification of Ukraine and the *Holodomor*

Joseph Stalin held the Communist Party of the Soviet Union in an iron grip from Lenin's death in 1924, until his own death in 1953. His ruthless ambition established him as an absolute dictator by 1937, calling the shots in the politburo, the highest decision making structure in the USSR.

All over its territories, the Communist Party had idealistically established communal farms to boost production. It was not so simple, however. Shortages began to bite everywhere in the USSR. Millions of Ukrainians were exterminated by targeted famine in the winter of 1932-1933.

*Holodomor* means "murder by hunger."

Stalin's politburo blacklisted farms and villages in Ukraine. Nobody was allowed to leave home to go looking for food. Anything that *did* grow on Ukrainian farms was taken away to feed Russians in distant cities. That winter, official raiding parties requisitioned anything edible from every farmhouse and village. Ukrainians died in droves in the countryside, and were buried in mass graves.

Five million people died of hunger in the USSR that year, about four million of whom were Ukrainians. The politburo suppressed the 1937 census figures for Ukraine to mask their actions, but counting back from subsequent population statistics, there is a horrendous hole in the Ukrainian population. The urban populations were shielded by rationing, controlled by ration cards. Corpses of the starved nevertheless appeared frequently on city pavements.

Secret police arrested and executed or imprisoned people indiscriminately. The gulags, Russian detention and labor camps that were run to control dissenters, filled up with Ukrainians. Friendly respect of Ukrainian culture came to a sudden halt, and Moscow reigned through raw terror. Officials ceased to even pretend to use Ukrainian, and if you wanted to survive, you made yourself sound very Russian in public.

During this winter, the USSR exported a million tons of wheat to the west.

However, neither Russia's charm offensive nor genocide persuaded Ukrainians that they were suddenly ordinary Russian peasants. Ukrainians' self belief proved invulnerable.

## Industrialization of Ukraine

Stalin's vicious repression led to a cessation of opposition in Ukraine. His military and policing interventions were shockingly effective in bringing about compliance. Once the communists had pacified Ukraine in this way, mining and industry sectors began to churn out profits—for the USSR. Stalin quickly rebuilt the industrial network of Ukraine that had been destroyed by war. Starting with coal and iron mining, Ukrainian industry branched out into electricity generation. Steel works and machinery fabrication grew, as well as chemical production and food processing.

These industries provided some employment and local infrastructure development, but in a Soviet Union, everything gets taken away to be shared out. The politburo was never particularly generous in redistributing resources it had taken from it back to Ukraine. Ukraine's economy did develop, but very slowly.

In 1941, it came to an abrupt halt.

## Ukraine During the Second World War

During WWII, Ukraine was raked over by opposing armies yet again. In 1941, Nazi Germany invaded Russia. The efficient Nazi war machine had control of all of Ukraine by November of that year. They found that the Soviets had destroyed crops and flooded mines as they retreated, and generally made the land unlivable. Unfortunately, that also made the land inhospitable to Ukrainians.

At first, the Ukrainians cheered on the Nazis as liberators from Russia. The American-published newspaper *Svoboda* was banned for a while in Canada for being so pro-Nazi. *Svoboda*'s editorial policy changed, though, as news began to filter back about the behavior of the most recent occupiers of Ukraine. A hopeful "Provisional Ukrainian State" was savagely suppressed within days. Ukraine was divided up again between Poland and Romania, and the Nazi *Reichskommissariat Ukraine.*

The Nazis efficiently murdered 1.5 million Ukrainian Jews over the next four years. The hated collective farms were left in place, now under German management. Ukrainian wheat was on the move yet again, this time back west to Germany. Shockingly, more than two million Ukrainians were conscripted as slave-workers for fields and factories of Germany.

The Ukrainian Orthodox Church was the only legal Ukrainian organization left. There *were* networks of communist cells and Ukrainian activist cells, but they had limited firepower and organizational capacity. By the end of the war, the Ukrainian Insurgent Army—the *Ukrayins'ka povstans'ka armiya*—had fought against the Soviet Union, the Poles, and the Nazis. The prevailing sentiment among underground political groups moved sharply away from fascist nationalism, and began to articulate a longing for a democratic and inclusive way of government.

In 1943, the Russians defeated the Germans at Stalingrad, and began to push westward again. By October 1944, they had painstakingly retaken all of Ukraine. The Nazis, as *they* retreated, burned and blew up fields and infrastructure. The

Ukrainians were once more left on the ashes of a battlefield. They went into the war with a population of about 45 million. At the cessation of hostilities, they were down to about 36 million. At least five million people had been killed, and about four million displaced. In all, 700 urban centers and 28,000 villages had to be rebuilt from rubble (Encyclopedia Britannica, 2022).

During WWII, Ukraine's borders were redrawn by the communists (who had taken Eastern Europe). Any Polish people in Galicia-Volhynia were forcibly relocated to Poland, and any Ukrainians in Poland were dumped into the chaos of post-war Galicia-Volhynia. Another significant purge was that Stalin deported the entire population of Tatar peoples from Crimea, leaving the land depopulated.

After the latest weary war, though, Ukrainians still wanted the same thing—freedom. *Svoboda.*

**Key Takeaways**

- Products of Ukrainian agriculture, mining, and industry were diverted from Ukraine to Russia.
- Lenin opted for allowing Ukraine a certain amount of cultural and linguistic freedom.
- Stalin reversed Lenin's policy by violently suppressing any sign of Ukrainian nationalism, going as far as to starve millions of Ukrainians to death.
- Stalin continued Russia's program of replacing Ukrainians with Russians in Ukraine.

- Industrialization in Ukraine was under the control of Russia.
- During the Second World War, Ukraine was a continuous battlefield for Nazi Germany and Russia.
- Many Ukrainians fought in the armies of the USSR.

It is easy to paint yourself as a "liberator" if you can help to establish a half-way credible internal party that calls for your "help." But ruling the "reluctantly liberated" is not easy. Russia discovered (to the cost of Ukrainians) that fancy theory about farming does not make for efficient agriculture.

The yearning for independence is not an insignificant aspect of national culture. Nations who do not have their own national integrity cannot be fobbed off with flattery, threats, or gifts. People will die for independence. Oppressed people do not easily forget or forgive inhumane treatment, no matter how closely you control the media and the history books.

Oppression, starvation, torture, and death had poisoned the soil, but still the wheat sprouted, and still the powerful Ukrainian peasants shouldered their burdens and scraped a living off the land. The history of Ukraine is the history of suffering and endurance.

# Chapter 6. Ukraine After Stalin—Khrushev's "Thaw" 1953-1990

(Grabowska, 2020)

*"Ideas are far more powerful than guns. We don't let our people have guns. Why should we let them have ideas?" — Joseph Stalin* (Stalin, n.d.)

As the world got rapidly more crowded and interconnected, it began to become more difficult to pull off a feat like hiding the *Holodomor*. The global mood was becoming more resistant to arbitrary war. The League of Nations of 1920 was followed by the United Nations in 1945, both organizations formed by a consensus among many nations that it would be better to conduct global affairs through peaceful discussion rather than war. The Ukrainian SSR was one of the 51 founding signatories. At least there has been some semblance of peer pressure against great crimes of state. As the world opened up to view, the attention of the world was drawn to hidden genocides and invasions, and Ukraine became a textbook case in the political theory classes of the world's universities.

## Stalin's Dying Days

Blow still followed blow in Ukraine, however. Immediately after WWII, between 1946 and 1947, drought, infrastructure loss, and famine on the burnt wheatlands killed almost another million Ukrainians. Stalin was back, too, and his mood had not improved. In Stalin's mind, Ukraine could best serve the interests of the USSR by the rapid rebuilding of heavy industry. Russian investment made that happen. Agriculture crept back from wartime devastation much more slowly. Ukraine became a region of smoking chimneys and ration cards.

It also became a land of shadows and fear, as a relentless crackdown was set in motion by the secret police. Anyone caught expressing pro-Ukrainian sentiments was exiled. Anybody who had was adjudged to have collaborated with the Nazis, was shot, or sent off to labor camps. Any synagogues which survived the Holocaust were demolished under an anti-Jewish drive. Slave laborers repatriated from Nazi Germany were mostly sent straight off to the gulags to do further slave labor, this time for their Soviet comrades.

The Ukrainian Greek Catholics and Ukrainian Orthodox Church were forced to combine and join the Russian

Orthodox Church. Another clade of underground resistance groups in the form of disaffected Christians arose instantly, but Stalin seemed content that he had stamped out all Ukrainianism in the Church.

Stalin decreed that poets, playwrights, and authors should stop harping on about the past glories of Ukrainians, and instead produce works admiring the Russians, and celebrating the USSR. It's hard to see how this would go over with a deeply partisan Ukrainian public, but I guess if Stalin told you to clap, you clapped very enthusiastically.

Stalin believed that the way to get Ukrainians to forget their Ukrainian roots and merge seamlessly into the USSR was to force everyone to speak Russian. Administration was conducted in Russian. High schools and universities had to function in Russian. The content of all levels of education was minutely controlled, to avoid exploration of other-than-socialist ideas. Tertiary education was made deliberately difficult for Ukrainians to enter. Unless you held Communist Party membership, you could not study further.

As he grew older, Stalin grew increasingly paranoid. He accused his physicians of a plot against him. Perhaps he was right. He abruptly died on March 5th, 1953, joining the tens of millions of USSR citizens he had exterminated.

## Crimea Handed Over to Ukraine 1954

Nikita Khrushchev inherited Stalin's USSR. The Russian-led Soviet Socialist Republics had developed into a formidable force on the world stage. A Soviet atom bomb was developed and tested, and Russia became fully nuclear capable—the first H-bomb test was in October of the year Stalin died.

Stalin had ruled the politburo without opposition. The 13 "other-than-Russian" Soviet Republics, like Ukraine, had been battered and starved and exploited. Khrushchev realized he had to do something radical to avert rebellion. He set a massive "de-Stalinization" process in motion, trying to defuse the dangerous cult that had grown up around his megalomaniac predecessor. In the case of Ukraine, he decided that a magnanimous gesture was needed.

So, after centuries of abject suffering, something rather miraculous happened in Ukraine. Russia gave Crimea back in 1954. Russia had taken the Crimean Peninsula off the Turks in 1783, who had in turn taken it the Kyivan Rus' centuries before. Ever since the Russian annexation, it had been administered by a dozen or so administrations. It was like a bolt rattling around inside an engine for the politburo. The politburo wanted to repopulate Crimea—Stalin's post-war ethnic cleansing of Crimean Tatars had left it severely underpopulated and unproductive. In addition, giving a large piece of territory to Ukraine might have been intended as a plaster on wounds left by Stalin (although it remained treasonable to even mention the *Holodomor*).

Whatever the reason, everything was duly approved and signed off, and Ukraine took final, permanent possession of the Crimean Peninsula. It's important to stress this, given events that unfolded in 2014.

**Walking Back the Stalin Years**

The USSR desperately needed a more humane face if it was to have any hope of staying together after Stalin. As with any charismatic and brutal strongman throughout history, as soon as the dreaded ruler dies, the forcibly united peoples of his empire immediately start agitating for their freedom. Khrushchev had been the leader of the Ukrainian SSR before he won the succession battle for head of the Russian State and head of the USSR. He had established a reputation as being a reasonable leader. He certainly did not display the anti-Ukrainian xenophobia of Stalin.

Khrushchev was quick to get rid of Stalin's henchman, Melnikov, the First Secretary of the Communist Party of Ukraine, and replace him with Kyrychenko, an actual Ukrainian! Kyrychenko came from the historically pro-Russian eastern edge of Ukraine. He was, nonetheless, undeniably Ukrainian. Khrushchev tasked him with reversing the Stalinist approach by appointing Ukrainian administrators and reintroducing Ukrainian language courses (and Ukrainian academics) in the universities. This seemed to appease the Ukrainian public.

People developed a grudging acceptance of the new administration, and young Ukrainians began to join the Ukrainian Communist Party in unprecedented numbers. Ukraine had one million Communist Party cardholders in 1958—about 60% of whom were Ukrainian. It was a no-brainer. If you wanted to get an office job, you had to join the Party. How loyal these new yuppy conscripts would be to the USSR was a moot point.

Khrushchev was not a Ukrainian hero, however. He inherited Lenin's arrogant dismissal of religion. From the viewpoint of an astute politician, he recognized alternative power and authority structures when he saw them. An unofficial "five-year-plan" from 1960-1965 saw thousands of Orthodox Churches closed. Religion was removed from the everyday world of ordinary Ukrainians, and Khrushchev anticipated that this would facilitate widespread conversion to communism.

## The Thaw

Khrushchev made his famous "secret speech" in 1956 to a closed session of the Communist Party, in which he shredded Stalin's personality cult. He argued that Stalin had been too full of ego to rule effectively, since nobody dared to contradict him. It was too easy to simply get shot. Khrushchev only addressed specifically Russian concerns in his speech, ignoring the possibility that Ukraine might have its own unique grievances against Stalin. He criticized Stalin's excesses, as they had proved disastrous for Russia at different points of WWII, and subsequently. He denounced the use of torture to gain "confessions." Everybody in the party seemed keen to move on. Khrushchev, however, did not draw attention to the savagery of the Stalinist years in Ukraine or elsewhere in the Sputnik (satellite) states.

Khrushchev released most of the Ukrainians imprisoned in northern gulags under a 1956 amnesty. Hundreds of thousands returned home—some enforced slave laborers, who had first been in Nazi Germany and then immediately in the Russian gulags, had lost more than a decade of their lives. Many more had left and died. Nothing could atone for such monstrosity, so Khrushchev tried to put some time and a lot of media control between them and the Stalin era, hoping for people to forget. The problem was that

Ukrainians had centuries of practice in remembering injuries.

Ukranians sprang into action immediately, once the pressure was lifted. Writers began to write all the poems, plays, novels, and histories that would have had them sent to Stalin's labor camps a handful of years previously. Heroes who had published under Stalin's reign were awarded medals and honors (sometimes posthumously). Ukrainian leaders who had been exiled and imprisoned by Stalin were freed and repatriated. An academic journal devoted to Ukrainian history was published—and *not* immediately banned!

## Stagnation and Attempts at Reform

The Communist Party of Ukraine has always been a propaganda product. It was never created by an uprising of the peasants and working classes in order to topple a capitalist oppressor class, as per spec in Marx's theory. It was simply the latest in a long line of foreign controllers, established through manipulating internal political processes.

In 1964 Khrushchev was deposed, and Leonid Brezhnev ascended to the "iron throne" of the USSR. These were the days of the nuclear race, with world powers jockeying to gain a big enough nuclear stick to discourage anyone else dropping bombs on them—or interfering with their internal affairs, for that matter. A proxy war between Russia and the USA was launched in Southeast Asia. Cosmonauts battled astronauts for the press coups of space exploration. Ukraine faded into the background, into a few blessed years of relative peace. The nation was still smoldering internally, however, like a cargo of coal that had caught fire, but the ship of state was sailing on with at least nominal steerage.

Brezhnev followed a policy of letting sleeping dogs lie in Ukraine, which was fulfilling its grain, coal and steel quotas, so it could be ignored. New hydroelectric dams produced irrigation for the wheatlands, and electricity for the towns and industries. Everybody in Ukraine was (officially) housed in a heatable flat. However, development stalled at the point of its usefulness to the USSR, and Ukraine fell into economic stagnation. Ukraine's gas was piped to Europe, for instance, but Europe paid *Moscow* for the supplies. Ukraine had to buy back its own gas.

Brezhnev was a great builder of mythical statues in Ukraine. All of them had a sort of xenophobic rationale that appealed to visiting Russian dignitaries—*Look how much Ukraine admires Russia!*—but failed to impress patriotic Ukrainians. Russian statues in Ukraine were intended to dominate the landscape in the way that the Russians wished to dominate the soul of the Ukrainians. Brezhnev's vast 100 meter tall concrete and stainless steel depiction of *Rodina Mat* ("Mother Motherland"), erected in Kyiv in 1981 from 700 tons of Ukrainian steel, does not mean to the Ukrainians what the Russians wish it meant. Ukrainians call it "Brezhnev's Daughter," and it stirs the desire for freedom in every patriot whenever they catch a glimpse of it.

**The Immigrants**

Over the centuries, nobody much *wanted* to immigrate into Ukraine. Only the Ukrainians loved Ukraine, but they were not allowed its free use. This trend continued until the 1950s, when a new stream of Russian workers flooded the industrial regions of Eastern Ukraine. About eight million Russians made their home in Ukraine after WWII.

This was not a spontaneous migration. Ukranians were deported en masse (but in small parcels) to various northern Soviets. Deprived of their language, religion, and education in these new destinations, their relatively small numbers were quickly assimilated into their new host cultures. At the same time, the monolithically Russian body of settlers and laborers was channeled into Ukraine. Russian language, education, and religion were all fostered by the Russian-controlled Ukrainian administration. The stated objective, once again, was to Russify Ukraine. The Donets Basin region (the so-called Donbas) became overwhelmingly Russian.

By the time of the dissolution of the Soviet Union in 1991, Ukraine's Russian population had reached about 22%. Russia had succeeded in loading Ukraine with a Russian power-bloc. These deliberate modifications of demographics opened up options for manipulation and control of the political processes of neighboring states that have subsequently proved very useful to Vladimir Putin's expansionist ambitions.

### The Ukrainian Diaspora

*Voluntary* emigration from Ukraine was also a major factor. Millions of people who self-identify as Ukrainians live in Ukrainian-cultured communities around the globe. Tactical Russian dispersals have located large Ukrainian communities in many of the post-Soviet countries: Russia, Kazakhstan, Moldova, and Belarus have crowds who wave the Ukrainian blue-and-yellow at sports matches. Canada, Poland, and the United States each have more than a million ethnic Ukrainians.

Those who found their way to other parts of the world were able to establish cultural support for émigré Ukrainians. The World Congress of Free Ukrainians was founded in the US in 1967, to the horror of the USSR press. An Institute of Ukrainian Studies was set up at Harvard. Although Ukrainians abroad mostly worked in mining and agriculture, many leading thinkers and political figures found their way to places where they could agitate on behalf of their *Rodina*. Ukrainian communities provided welcome, shelter, and logistical support for advocates on behalf of a free Ukraine. Family links count for a lot in raising funds to help change the status quo in a distant motherland.

Pogroms against Jews had been a sporadic horror in Ukraine down the centuries, long before the Nazi holocaust. Ukrainian Jews fled to many places, but since 1991 with the reduction of travel restrictions, more than a quarter of a million have made their way to Israel. This is one reason for the struggles Ukraine has had with its economy. The Jews have been subjected to harassment through the centuries, and they have developed religious and economic strategies for surviving and thriving under duress. If a nation loses its Jewish population, it loses a whole sector of vital community capacity.

## Key Takeaways

- Stalin tried to destroy Ukrainian culture and make all Ukrainians feel that they were Russians—but Ukrainian literature and religion thrived underground.
- Khrushchev reversed Stalin's policy of enforced "russification" and tried to erase the memories of his atrocities.
- In 1954, Russia gave Crimea back to Ukraine.
- Khrushchev released hundreds of thousands of Ukrainians from the Russian gulags.
- Brezhnev continued to allow some cultural and linguistic freedoms to Ukrainians, but continued to encourage Russians to migrate to Ukraine.

It is not easy to erase national consciousness by forcibly submerging it in an oppressive culture, and large scale atrocities cannot be propagandized away. If too many people die, it leaves an indelible wound in the cultural psyche of the oppressed, and as media and international scrutiny develop technology for uncovering facts, national propaganda loses its effectiveness.

It becomes clear as we look at the history of Ukraine that a centralized government of a state consisting of many unique cultures can only work if meaningful participation and self-determination of all participants is allowed.

# Chapter 7. Ukraine—Free After Eight Centuries 1991-2022

(Blan, 2019)

"*Nowhere else did repressions, purges, suppressions, and all other kinds of bureaucratic hooliganism in general acquire such horrifying scope as in Ukraine, in the struggle against powerful forces concealed in the Ukrainian masses that desired more freedom and independence.*" *—Leon Trotsky* (Trotsky, 2021)

It had been 800 years since Ukraine had last conducted its own affairs. In this chapter, we will look into the remarkable "freedom by default" that Ukraine was gifted with at the end of the Soviet era.

## The Real Dominos: The Soviet Union's Sudden

## Collapse

At the dawn of the 1980s, General Secretary Mikhail Gorbachev was struggling desperately to keep the great USSR together. The public and international rhetoric was as self-confident as always, but more hollow than ever. In the USA, a key plank of the American Vietnam War propaganda had been the fear of the "domino effect," an inexorable one-by-one collapse of Southeast Asian nations to communist onslaught. The real domino-collapse came at the end of the 1980s, and not in Southeast Asia.

The much vaunted solidarity of the Soviets began to look rather ragged. Political conflicts between the satellite Soviets and the Russian "mothership" began to grow serious. Gorbachev did not have Stalin's stomach for brutal repression. Conflict grew into full blown nationalist agendas. It turned into a game of *dare*.

Estonia was the first Soviet socialist republic to declare itself a sovereign state in 1988, carefully hedging its bets by asserting its intention to remain in close fellowship. No reprisals happened. No armies were mobilized. Lithuania went next, declaring its independence from the Union in 1990. Southern caucasus and Georgia pulled within two months, and the entire Baltic region was out.

In 1991, an internal coup of horrified Russian hardliners failed to topple Gorbachev or halt the crumbling of Moscow's power. Within the next few months, many of the remaining 11 Soviets pulled the trigger on the departure clause. Gorbachev was compelled by events to recognize the independence of the Baltic states in September 1991. The dominoes continued to go clattering down.

President Yeltsin of Russia, Chairman Shushkevich of Belarus, and President Kravchuk of Ukraine signed the Belavezha Accords on the 8th of December that year, and the USSR was almost gone. Kazakhstan was the last to depart, and that was it. No more USSR.

After all the relentless propaganda, after all the tortured confessions and executions, after all the extra-judicial murders and callous imprisonments, and after all the cruel exile of anybody who was the least suspicion of heterodoxy, the USSR was no more. The world was in shock. Russia was in shock. The battered former subaltern Soviets were filled with fierce nationalistic joy.

## The Troubled Transition to 30 Years of Peace

The *Rada* had proposed a Ukrainian Declaration of Independence in August 1991. A referendum ratified it by a more than 90% "yes" vote on December 1st. A week later, Ukraine was officially on its own.

For the *first* time in eight *centuries*.

For the Ukrainian nationalists, it was a day of long awaited jubilation: Free at last! For the Russians, it was a deep humiliation. *Slava Ukraine!* sang the gleeful, newly released Ukrainians—*Glory to Ukraine*. Everyday Russians were bewildered by so much happiness. Russia released its grip on Ukraine with the same reluctance that the Western European states granted freedom to their African colonies.

The Warsaw Pact nations and Baltics immediately joined NATO. That caused instant alarm in Russia and those nations that remained aligned to it. To make tensions deeper, Ukraine (along with Moldova and Georgia) started showing interest in joining NATO too. This would become an important part of Putin's defense of his moves on Ukraine.

## Ukraine in the Age of Globalization

Globalization means that nations and cultures have achieved an unprecedented functional closeness with intensified openness among cultures and nations. It is mediated by all the systems of culture—education, medicine, commerce, technology, religion, communication, policing, and all the rest. In our world of seven billion and more human beings, we are more tightly thrown together than ever before.

The impact of the "new normal" of global interconnectedness has had different effects on dominant cultures as opposed to dominated cultures. These effects are well illustrated by the case of Russia and Ukraine.

### *Social Media and Propaganda in Ukraine*

Russia has lost its capacity to isolate millions of people from each other, and stop them from forming alternative interpretations of events on the ground. The propaganda machine can no longer be sure that Russians or Ukrainians are only hearing the carefully curated state version of reality. Ordinary Ukrainians can now see images of Russian tanks in flames. Since the late 1990s, it has become impossible to prevent people from exploring different sources of media information. The first politicization of the new non-official media was during the "Arab Spring" of 2011, when social media became the vehicle for revolutionaries in North Africa. Ukraine took note.

Repressive regimes around the world have quickly realized that state media is losing its power, and have moved into the social media space with more sophisticated propaganda-by-volume tactics. Humans can weaponize anything, even their cell phones.

However, two can play that game, and Ukrainians are big players in the cybersphere.

### *Globalized Technology and Commerce in Ukraine*

Ukraine's economy has always been kept simple—it produces wheat, gas, and steel for Russia to use in the global capitalism market. The irony is that we have had *communists* exerting *vassalage* on Ukraine in order to compete on *global markets.* Marx would have been scratching his beard worriedly in the British Library.

Over the last brief quarter-century, Ukraine has had to build an independent economy for the first time in eight centuries. It has not been easy. For instance, the Ukrainian gas company (unimaginatively called Ukrtransgaz), is in an uneasy partnership with Russia and Belarus. From Russia's point of view, Ukraine is in a dangerously strong position. It's hard to drive good deals if somebody else can just turn off a tap, although in fact, Russia itself turned the taps off back in 2006. Wars have been fought over less, and gas has emerged as a factor in the most recent conflict.

The economy of Ukraine has not been booming, although it has shown promise in a few small areas. Agriculture is back on track, with the black soil doing what it has always done—and for the first time, Ukraine has had the luxury of deciding who it sells its wheat to, and at what price. The problem lies in a stagnant industrial and mining sector, still heavily under the influence of conservative management. The strong pro-Russian sentiment of the Donbas region has not motivated energetic devotion to the economic cause of Ukraine.

The broadening of the scope of its industries is vital for the long-term prosperity of Ukraine. However, development is obstructed by poor relations with its powerful northern neighbor. War—and the threat of war—do not build investor confidence. Ukraine not only needs self-determination, it also needs peace.

The tourism sector is the quintessential "new" industry of the globalizing world. Enormous profits are derived from people visiting one another's countries briefly to enjoy its unique features. Tourism monetizes temporary travel and human curiosity. It also establishes the importance of the unique. Nobody ever wanted to visit a Ukrainian factory—but many tourists want to canoe in Ukrainian rivers and sunbathe on the white beaches of the Black Sea. Tourism is both a symbol of globalization and a vehicle for it.

A quick check on the internet reveals that there are 660,000 Ukrainian beach-side hotels. There is also currently a warning that it is currently unsafe to make bookings for an Odessa holiday. The hotel boom demonstrates the market for sunshine among people living in the chilly north. This is one of the new products and services that could become a driver in an emerging economy.

### *Religion, Globalization, and Ukraine*

When the USSR dispersed, a survey on religious affiliation showed that only 39% of Ukrainians considered themselves religious. Of course, it might depend on who is asking, and how clever it might be to admit to having faith of any sort. Atheism was official dogma, taught as the "whole truth" in schools. Being outed as religious was very bad for your employment or advancement prospects.

It was a well-worn tactic—successive Russian regimes had tried to control the Ukrainian soul. The USSR was not officially hostile to people holding faith, but it insisted that Ukrainian Orthodox Christians be led by a Russian metropolitan in Russia, who had everything to lose if he failed to toe the pro-Soviet line. That was not popular. Nevertheless, a stubborn 39% of Ukrainians were determined to tell a Russian census-taker that they were Christian.

By 2015, poll numbers put self-identification as Christian at 78%!

There are different ways cultures react to globalizing pressure. Ukrainians could have simply assimilated to Russian culture, as intended by the politburo. Many did. Or Ukrainians could have fled to some place where they could maintain their Ukrainian identity. Again, many did. Or Ukrainians could become secret believers, hiding their true faith and nationalism. The Ukrainian who chose that response held a nationalism tied to religion at the deepest level. Everything else could be stripped away, but you could live and die as a Ukrainian Orthodox believer.

The Church had proved itself by suffering alongside its people. It handed out the most abject defeat to Russia's social engineering attempts. Religion might be on the decline in Western Europe, but it's the opposite in Ukraine. The power of the Church is that it is the most Ukrainian thing in Ukraine.

## *The Rise of the Global Criminals*

Hoards of "forgotten" guns and ammunition were left stockpiled in Ukraine after 1991. The Ukrainian mob started as gun-runners, forming disciplined militaristic organizations, much like the original Cossacks. They were not interested in Ukrainian nationalism. Their interest was in running clandestine trade for wealth.

The AK47s and their short 7.62 ammunition found their way into West Africa and Afghanistan. People running wars paid top-price for battle-tested Ukrainian hardware. The mob made a killing. They branched out naturally into narcotics and people-trafficking. Their tentacles reached all over the world in the shadow economies of the nations, trading anything, even something as apparently innocuous as cigarettes.

These cartels operate a parallel economy in Ukraine, sapping the energy of the open economy through buying corrupt influence. The Ukrainian mafia thrives best where the rule of law is not enforced or enforceable, and therefore prefers war to peace. The underworld connects seamlessly across nations, and it is from these dark roots that the oligarchs emerge, who have real political power—which is why they are being pressured by Ukraine's allies.

## Key Takeaways

- Russia had never wanted Ukraine to be independent from it. The 1991 dissolution of the USSR was widely regarded by the Russians as a great disaster.
- New technologies result in new ways of waging war.
- None of the world's faiths simply go away in the face of opposition. Religion is a powerful social institution which promotes self-identity.
- Many nefarious interest groups in Ukraine do not actively want peace.

It is an innovation of our times for a nation to have aspirations to independence *without* dominating any other territory. The consensus of the world's nations is that countries should be self-determining and interdependent (without domination/subordination). Many nations, like Ukraine, are calling for fair treatment, a dynamic which is open to manipulation by external interests, who might want to encourage *separation* of countries into smaller states which would then "align" themselves favorably with neighboring territories. Russia, for one.

In the next chapter, we shall examine how nationalistic bias intersects with our human search for peace, as we discuss the search for an unbiased version of history.

# Chapter 8. Fighting Over Facts—What Really Happened in Ukraine?

(Kuzmina, 2022)

*"The very ink with which history is written is merely fluid prejudice."* —Mark Twain (Khurana, 2017)

Watching the same news broadcast on TV on two different channels gives us a foretaste of how differently history will be told by different sides. Fox will broadcast what the President said; CNN will focus on how he stumbled down the ramp. Both sides are presenting "the truth," *what really did happen*—but each side curates what is most advantageous to their particular worldview. That is "*bias*." At times, however, different sides tell outright lies. That is "*propaganda*." All we can do as investigators of the past is to work out which side distorted the truth *less*.

I will now take a closer look into the claims and counter-claims of Ukrainian nationalists and Russian imperialists. Then I will draw certain conclusions, which is where the discussion between historians begins.

## The Control of History

Every Ukrainian is a historian. When all the media and all the school history textbooks tend one way, then "history" becomes a subject of popular conversation. *Alternative* history. It doesn't take a genius, especially a Ukrainian with a nationalistic grudge, to spot that Ukrainians are being offered a Russian perspective on history.

There are many narrators of the Ukrainian story. Telling the story from a Ukrainian viewpoint was a punishable offense during much of history. The Poles wanted it told one way, and the Ottomans another. Cossacks, Germans, and Russians all had their way of seeing and justifying their presence in Ukraine. The Kyivan Rus' themselves had swept in under Oleg in the 700s, so there must be other stories plowed under the soil of Ukraine, and drowned in its marshes. Our origin myths of "unoccupied territory" forget the bones of the tribes that our invading ancestors buried. Nevertheless, the gift of the adult is to say *stop fighting*, and *give her back her toy*. In our fragile world, we are desperate to stop our deadly bickering. If we do not stop at some *point in history*, then we will never stop.

Here are two versions of the story of Ukraine side-by-side. You will already know where my bias lies. I shall, however, try to give both sides a hearing, and at least show where a reader might go to follow their own confirmation bias. The same word in both Russian and Ukrainian—правда (*pravda*)— translates as "truth."

## Competing Historical Memories—Ukraine versus Russia

The monuments in Ukraine say one thing. The memory of Ukrainians says another.

### *The Heritage of Kyivan Rus'*

Who are the true heirs of Kyivan Rus'? The Russians claim the name with some credibility. Ukraine has always been "Russian" since the Swedish Rus' invaded and populated the area from 500-700 CE, but they did not use the name of themselves. They were the first Russian speakers, although they have always called their language Ukrainian.

It was Ivan the Terrible/Formidable (depending on how you translate *grozny*) who proclaimed himself "Tsar of all Rus'" or the Tsar of Russia, in 1547. Until then, he had been merely the Grand Prince of Moscow. When Russian students read history now, they assume that Ivan was also Tsar of Ukrainian Rus'.

Ukrainian readers of the same history claim that just because a prince in Moscow said he was King of the Rus' did not make him King of Ukrainian Rus'. Kyiv was not a part of Ivan's empire. Russians had to painstakingly wrest control of Ukraine over the following centuries. Kyivan Rus' still exists, and it is still occupied by those who speak a language forged on its soil. Rulers have come and gone, but Ukrainians are still where Ukrainians should be.

For a Muscovite Russian, that is irrelevant. Ukraine is a fringe Russian-cultured land that has a natural cultural connection to the great Russian Empire. *Why are they making such a fuss about an issue that was decided by Ivan the Formidable?*

*That psychopath, who lost more than he gained, and killed his own son?* the Ukrainians respond. *Ukraine was never part of his brutal empire.*

### ***Hetman Ivan Mazepa—Traitor or National Hero?***

Ivan Mazepa, the Russian-appointed Cossack Hetman ("headman" or "general") of Eastern Ukraine, was one of the wealthiest men in Europe. He was one of those outsider rulers who realized you could achieve profitable stability through respect for culture.

He was also an opportunistic politician. In 1687, he accused his *Hetman* predecessor of anti-Russian sympathies, and got him toppled. The Tsar liked to see such pro-Russian sentiments, and appointed him the next *Hetman*. Mazepa then began to amass land and wealth, and to dispense largesse. He built countless Orthodox churches. He expanded the Kyiv University.

Then, in 1702, Polish-Cossack *Hetman* Semen Paliy in the western provinces revolted against their Polish overlords, and Mazepa persuaded Tsar Peter I to let him help his fellow Cossack. Permission granted, Western Ukraine reverted to Cossack-Russian rule. Subsequently, however, Tsar Peter refused to send Russian reinforcements when the Polish threatened to take it back again in 1708. So, Mazepa decided to drop Russia and join the Swedish-Polish alliance.

Mazepa was killed in battle. The Cossacks were slaughtered in a widespread ethnic cleansing. The Russian Orthodox Church anathematized Mazepa, and that curse has never yet been lifted. In Russian eyes, Mazepa will always be a traitor to the *Rodina.*

Mazepa became a default martyr to the Ukrainian people. Ukrainians remember him as a leader who united Ukraine and died for it. The Russian curse is still in place, but loyal Ukrainians revere Mazepa as a hero. The Communist Party always portrays him as an arch-villain. It is only recently that statues of Mazepa have started to be installed in public places in Ukraine.

### *Lenin—Founder or Oppressor of the Ukrainian State?*

On the other side of the balance sheet is Vladimir Ilyich Lenin. A Ukrainian history student would tell you to take all the great things said about Lenin in Russian History textbooks—and believe the opposite. Ukrainians are infuriated by the suggestion that just because Russia under Lenin fought others for control of their territories, he should be considered as the "founder" of the Ukrainian State. No bulky statues will persuade a Ukrainian that Lenin was not a bandit like all the rest.

Ordinary *Russians*, however, see things in a different light. "Ukraine" had been a patchwork of feuding provinces, unable to maintain stable statehood. Russian forces under Lenin federalized the Ukrainian regions which then became one of the three first signatories of the USSR. Lenin had exercised god-like powers in bringing peaceful order out of violent chaos, and Ukraine owed her a debt of gratitude.

That difference in opinion is going to take more than a little talking through.

### *The Holodomor—Non-Event or Genocide by Starvation?*

What happened in the winter of 1932–1933 in Ukraine?

For more than 50 years, the official Russian line was that snow fell and potatoes got frozen in the ground. There had been two years of drought and poor harvests, but that is what happens in the countryside. Yes, many nomadic Kazakhs and Ukrainian peasants died as a result, which is sad, but not unusual. The new collectivist approach to farming was still being resisted by reactionary *kulaks*, and was not yet able to produce food as efficiently as it could. The worst that could be said is that Stalin's five-year plan met with a few administrative hitches.

Gareth Jones was the only reporter among the international press contingent in Moscow at the time who reported on the deaths of peasants in Ukraine. He was banned, and subsequently "disappeared" while on assignment in

Mongolia in 1935. The journalistic community has always assumed it was a Soviet secret police hit.

It was only in the fallout of the Soviet white-wash attempt of the 1986 Chernobyl nuclear power station melt-down, that Ukrainian writers were able to mention the *Holodomor*. By then, the Soviet propaganda machine was leaking all sorts of stories that it had buried. It was no surprise to Ukrainians. If four million people die in a single winter, too many millions of people carry memories.

A Ukrainian would never classify the *Holodomor* as an obscure seasonal tragedy. It is a hot memory of generation-crossing grievance that has become part of the universal Ukrainian consciousness.

### *Great Patriotic War—Who Was Patriotic to Which Motherland?*

In the one war, valiant Russian soldiers fought against the might of Nazi Germany to wrest Eastern Europe out of the tyrant's claw, in order to continue with their Russian-led quest for economic peace and equity among nations.

In the second war, just under half the Red Army consisted of Ukrainian peasants, who fought desperately and defeated the Nazis. More than 1.5 million Ukrainian soldiers received awards for courage. After victory, the Ukrainian battle-hardened peasant-soldiers were sent back to find peasantry things to do down in the backwoods of Ukraine.

In the third war, valiant Ukrainian soldiers fought a courageous guerilla war against the Nazi invasion, the

Polish invasion, and the Red Army invasion. For a few days they were able to enforce an independent Ukrainian Republic, which was savagely put down by Russian forces.

These were all the same war, known more widely as WWII.

The Russian official accounts ignore how many Ukrainians fought and died for the USSR cause. War monuments are everywhere in Ukraine—statues, tanks, and airplanes—each reinforcing the message of how grateful Ukrainians should be to their liberators. Russian tanks and heavy weapons in the 2022 invasion often carry a spray-painted "Z," a reminder of the black-and-orange striped George Cross ribbon given to so many heroes of the Great Patriotic War.

Ukrainian accounts are more concerned with how the Red Army, with all its Ukrainian soldiers, was deployed against the *Rodina* (the Ukrainian *Rodina*), to return the hated Russians to power.

Few say anything about the peasants with missing limbs and shell-shocked eyes. Their story is a great untold epic. Dispensable peasants fought for their overlords and their motherland, and were then forgotten. There are no Zs for fallen Ukrainians.

## ***Ukraine—Whole-Land Independence or Foreign Fragmentation?***

Ukrainian occupiers down the centuries have followed Caesar's maxim—*divide ut regnes* ("divide in order to control"). The logic is *Well, you got your independence, so why shouldn't Volhynia/Right Bank/Crimea/Donbas have theirs? How can you, of all nations, begrudge the aspirations to independence of another region?* While decrying Ukrainian nationalism, they have promoted micro-nationalism.

Ukrainians and Russians take different stances on whether that is gaslighting or not.

Russians see Ukraine as a complex mixture of Russian border-regions which have been alienated from their natural Russian roots. Ukrainian independence has been weaponized by the West to destabilize Russia. Economic sanctions and Ukraine's desire to join the EU are proof that Ukraine is a pawn in a global anti-Russian game. The West, with its lust for control of world resources, is the great predator.

This is different from the NATO countries' articulated understanding. For them, *Russia* is the great predator, hungry for control of Ukrainian resources. The Western nations simply want a "free market" in which they can bargain for the lowest possible prices for Ukrainian gas and wheat. Western media portray the West as the great gift-giver; the provider of arms and ammunition to the legitimate democratic state. No mention is made of any post-war friendship price-tag.

From a Ukrainian viewpoint, they acknowledge the tension between Russia and the West—but they want to avoid actual involvement. They desire independence, and are prepared to offer Ukrainian neutrality as an alternative to being the client state of *anybody*. After centuries of having their resources controlled and taken by others, they want peace in which to develop on their own.

## Key Takeaways

- Russia and Ukraine are locked in a battle about what really happened in Ukraine's history.
- Ukraine and Russia both claim to be the descendants of Kyivan Rus'.
- Ivan Mazepa tried to unite Ukraine as an independent state during the time of the Tsars—he is considered a villain by Russia, but a hero by Ukraine.
- Ukrainians remember the *Holodomor* as the murder of four million Ukrainians by Stalin. Russians consider it merely a seasonal famine.
- Russians remember the Second World War as the triumph of the USSR over Nazi Germany. Ukrainians are not acknowledged for their great role in the conflict.

History becomes really interesting to oppressed and exploited people—the more deeply polarized the different readings of history, the more likely conflict will develop. Attempting to bury evil deeds defers trouble to a later date. If the can is kicked far enough down the road, though, crimes become the concern of the archaeologist, rather than the politician.

In order to understand Ukraine's present realities, one has to understand its past realities, and specifically its relationships with Russia. The two nations will never find peace unless they can find some common ground in their contested history. In the next chapter, I will explore the granular differences that make peace so difficult.

# Chapter 9. Culture Wars—*Who* Is Ukraine?

(Альшин, 2020)

*"I would never want Ukraine to be a piece on the map, on the chessboard of big global players, so that someone could toss us around, use us as cover, as part of some bargain."*
*—Volodymyr Zelensky (2022)*

One of the functions of a robust culture is to empower its members to adapt to changes. Ukrainian culture has run underground for centuries, while the culture of Russia has dominated Ukraine. Now, Ukraine has had a short window to showcase itself—*as itself*—on the global stage. The story the Russians have been telling is not all there is to say about Ukraine.

In this chapter, we will take a look at how the cultural institutions of Ukraine differ from the official Russian myth of uniformity. We shall also see that one of the reasons for the strife over identity is that the two cultures *are in fact* very similar. Siblings squabble the hardest.

## Competing Cultural Institutions of Ukraine

A great area of contention in Ukraine is the role and importance of cultural institutions. Myths of origin are not simply fireside stories. They articulate a community's values, and express its aspirations. Cultural institutions exist to perpetuate the self-identity of a culture group.

We shall attempt to find our way into this subject by sitting down at a Ukrainian peasant's hearth, with a cup of hot, sweet tea grasped tightly in our chilly hands, listening to a classic folk tale that has come down through the shadows.

### *The Glorious Party or Iron Wolf?*

The Ukrainian folktale tells of a peasant who was helped to deal with a demonic "Iron Wolf" by his three talented dogs. As with many folktales, the symbolic coding of the politics of the oppressed are quite clear.

> *A* пресвітер *(presviter, or "clergyman") emancipated a long-serving servant, and gave him the gift of a magic egg in lieu of many years' wages. The Presviter explained that the peasant should go home, make a*

*cattle pen, and crack the egg inside it. He warned the peasant not to break it on the way home.*

*However, as happens in folk-tales, the peasant disobeyed this warning. Out streamed a great crowd of cattle, and the peasant was in despair as to how to herd them. Then up came the Iron Wolf and offered him a devilish bargain. The Iron Wolf would herd the cattle back into the egg, on condition that he would come and eat the peasant when he sat on the bridal bench.*

*The peasant agreed to this dubious bargain, and the Iron Wolf herded up the cattle and sealed them back in the egg. The peasant went back to his home village, built a cattle pen, and cracked the egg in it. It was immediately filled with cattle. He decided to farm with them, breeding and selling them, and he soon grew very rich.*

*One neighbor, a general, had a beautiful daughter. He asked the rich peasant to marry her. The peasant sadly told his story to the general, who offered to guard the church against the Iron Wolf with three ranks of soldiers. The wedding took place, but as soon as the peasant and his new bride sat down on the bridal bench, the Iron Wolf appeared! The three ranks of soldiers were no match for the monster, so the peasant jumped out a window and rode away into the forest on his horse, with the Iron Wolf close behind.*

*The peasant's horse was a good horse, and the wolf could not catch him. The man stopped at a hut and begged for shelter from its elderly owners. He warned them of the danger following him, but they told him they had a dog called Chutko, who could hear the wolf a mile off. So he lay down to sleep. In the night, Chutko barked, and the peasant raced away with the gift of a wheaten hearth-cake, as well as Chutko the dog. The Iron Wolf followed his tracks all day.*

*In the evening, the peasant stopped at another hut, and received the same hospitality and protection. The dog here was called Vazhko, and could hear pursuit nine miles off. When Vazhko barked in the night, the peasant escaped again, with the gift of a wheaten hearth-cake, and with Chatko and Vashko running alongside. The Iron Wolf followed at a distance, as before.*

*That evening, the peasant stopped at a third cottage. Exactly the same things happened, and he left with a wheaten hearth-cake and an additional dog, named Bary, who could hear the Iron Wolf from 12 miles away. The Iron Wolf's grim pursuit continued.*

*On the fourth evening, the peasant found himself at another hut, but this one was ominously empty. He lay down to sleep, with his three dogs on guard.*

*In the morning, the Iron Wolf came growling to the hut. Chutko barked! Vazhko pinned him to the ground! And Bary tore out his throat! Then the peasant rode home in safety to his new bride, followed by his three faithful dogs.*

Adapted from R. Nisbet Bain's translation of the original folktale (Bain, 2008).

Three guesses as to who the Iron Wolf is, children!

We have the whole history of Ukraine encoded in this grim little story. There is the blessing of freedom and prosperity that comes from serving the Orthodox Church. We have the unreasonable and devilish "help" offered by Lithuania/Poland/Russia—help with deadly strings attached. We have the rise of wealthy peasants so hated by Stalin, and the *Hetmancy* of the Cossacks failing to protect Ukraine. Then there is the relentless persecution of the Ukrainian peasants, down to the empty houses of the *Holodomor*. Finally, there is the apocalyptic vision of the tearing out of the Iron Wolf's throat, and we can all guess what that means too.

If the communist politicians had taken the time to listen to the folktales, they would not have been surprised at the Ukrainian joy over the dissolution of the USSR.

### *The Glorious Church or Foolish Superstition*

From an official communist viewpoint, religion is not only foolish, but dangerous. "Superstition" blunts the intellect, and prevents people from asking sociological questions about their condition. Religious leaders are often in cahoots with the bourgeoisie to maintain the stranglehold of elites. Religion, especially Christianity, softens the proletariat with talk of love and forgiveness, whereas the global workers' revolution needs them hot and vengeful. In Ukraine, this led to tactical shutting down of churches and intimidation of clergy. In 1918, the Bolsheviks executed the metropolitan of Kyiv. It was a bad time to be a public Christian.

For all its official disdain for religion, the communist politburo nonetheless recognized its power. At times they played the *You are a Russian religion, so God wants you to love Russia* card. Mostly, however, they relied on easy deterrents—demolition, imprisonment, and execution.

But the "exterminated" Church kept on resurrecting. The self-declared independent new offshoot, the Ukrainian Autocephalous Orthodox Church, gained many early Ukrainian adherents, but was brutally suppressed. Even Khrushchev was actively hostile. Thousands of Ukrainian churches closed in the first half of the 1960s. Outwardly, it appeared that Christianity was almost entirely broken, as a sociological factor in the politics of Ukraine.

With only *Pravda* on TV, ordinary Russians and Ukrainians understood that religion in Russia and Ukraine was failing, as people embraced science and Marxist theory. The myth of the inevitability of the People's Revolution was taught, enforced, and fostered. The spin-doctors of the Russian propaganda machine worked really hard to make it look like the theory was working out in actuality.

As soon as the grip of Russia began to slip, however, defiant Ukrainians began to voice their allegiance to the old Orthodoxy. Centuries of repression had taught Ukrainians how to *appear* to agree with overlords. Passive aggressive resistance is deeply ingrained in the Ukrainian psyche.

### *Russian Language versus Ukrainian Language*

For a Russian reader of Ukrainian history, Russian is the highly evolved language of science and literature. "Ukrainian language," on the other hand, is a rural proto-Russian creole, mixed with Polish and German, with no cultural value.

Ukrainian readers of history, however, consider Russian to be a dialect of *their* language. Ukrainians consider that they have developed a more cosmopolitan language, something like English. Russian is, for them, a tribal dialect grown too big for its limited roots and boots.

For the Russians, the Russian language is a potent unifying symbol system. It was the stamp of Russian supremacy branded on the flanks of the satellite states. The contemptuous haste with which the former Soviets dropped Russian and reinstated their local languages/dialects must have seemed like a slap in the face. Russians assumed that their allies were pleased to have education and government in the language of science and success, just as *Pravda* had been telling them. To the average Muscovite, the former satellites were guilty of gross ingratitude to the Russians, led astray by subversive Western propaganda.

### *News Media—Information on a Mission*

There is a fierce competition for the Ukrainian and Russian audiences. The role of "news" in the sort of situation that is currently engulfing the region is always broadcast as "information *with a purpose*."

- *It claims to be a truthful representation of facts*—Russian news agency *Pravda* faces the *Ukrainian* news agency *also* called *Pravda*. The pro-Russian RIA News observes that Russia has blown up 145 Ukrainian armored vehicles and more than 1200 tanks in the 2022 war between Russia and Ukraine. The 9GAG pro-Ukrainian website says that Ukraine only had 8 armored vehicles and 800 tanks to start with (9GAG, 2022). They cannot both be right (although they might both be wrong). Consumers of data make their own decisions based on pre-existing commitments.

- *It reassures people that their opinion is correct.* The much discussed "echo-chamber effect" refers to people consuming viewpoints with which they already agree. Broadcasters can thus nudge audiences to more extreme positions. One needs opinions to be as polarized as possible to sustain war.
- *It encourages people to continue fighting.* The motivational crisis-emotions of revulsion, hatred, fear, and rage need to be fed narrative fuel. The opposition is blamed for anything lurid and grisly, such as a child crucifixion or multiple rapes, to keep tempers flared.
- *It confirms people's trust in their leaders' decisions.* Favorable public opinion is essential to politicians, so one of their prime tasks is to boost the perceived validity of their leadership.
- *It seeks global support for one side of the conflict.* Global alliances are key in support of one's cause.

The TV channels, radio stations, online news channels, and newspapers are the nodes of information for which both sides contest. In 2021, Putin fired almost half of the staff of news outlet RIA Novosti, installing his own hand picked management team. An immediate priority of Russian invaders in Ukraine is to switch off Ukrainian news and replace it with Russian news. Ukrainians do the same when the war goes the other way. War is media war.

But does a media blitz persuade Ukrainians to accept Russian intervention? The Ukrainians have been playing the resistance-to-media game for centuries. Then again, the domination of the news-space is not necessarily aimed at Ukrainians, but at Russian public support for war.

If the 2022 war in Ukraine is truly a proxy war between Russia and the West, then who has not already picked an "echo chamber"? In terms of understanding what's happening in Ukraine, neither side is listening to the other. *A breakdown of communications* could almost be the definition of "war."

## *Monuments and Place Names*

Living near an imposing statue or monument, one ceases to notice it. It never impinges on one's thoughts. It is simply there. That does not mean to say that it has no significance—a statue's apparent invisibility is a sign that it has done its work by becoming an unchallenged part of local history.

Monuments and statues have a unique political voice. They are symbols of power and influence.

- *They claim those who made them were the only significant players in history*. In Ukraine, the "story" told by the vast statue of *Rodina Mat* is that Ukraine is only significant because Russia makes her so. It is a symbol of the insignificance of the self identity and independent value of Ukraine, literally overshadowed by the might of Russia. Everybody knows that it celebrates the Russian *Rodina* and not the Ukrainian *Rodina*.
- *They enforce the status quo of those who set them up*—those in power *then* are still in power *now*. They

are like weights on the tablecloth of Russian culture, and the Ukrainian table that holds them is not visible. The Russians want this "monumental lie" to become the background ideology of Ukraine; an unquestioned Russian view of history.

- *They teach communal values*—the person, event, or sentiment celebrated is intended to draw admiration and emulation. That is why Mazepa statues are hard to find in Ukraine.

In Kyiv there was, until very recently, an enormous sculpture depicting a Ukrainian and Russian worker dynamically upholding a sign of peace and mutual affection. In the heat of the rage against the Russian invasion of 2022, this monument was smashed to bits by angry Ukrainians. Centuries of passive aggression suddenly had a focus for public expression, and there is another story around the empty plinth—Russian power is gone, and we can step into its place. Bary has torn out the Iron Wolf's throat.

In 2015, the Ukrainian State went on an all-out counter-offensive against Soviet era statuary—a "decommunization" drive. There was a systematic targeting of Lenin statues in what was called the *Leninopad* or "Lenin-topple." Lenin's image was disfigured by having its nose cut off and statues were knocked down, relocated, or broken up for scrap.

## *Ukrainian Alienation from the Means of Production*

Karl Marx was a regular occupant of one of the tables in the newly built British Museum Reading Room. Throughout the 1860s, he scribbled away industriously, giving shape to his economic sociology. Marx believed that the rich become wealthy off the labor of the poor, and that the poor would inevitably revolt against such domination and establish a fair economy in which all would share alike in a global fraternity of nations.

The Ukrainian problem with Leninist-Stalinist Marxism was that yes, the wealthy and powerful elite were indeed exploiting the proletariat. The revolution had not ushered in a universal free sharing of resources, but simply a new elite who *talked* like peasants while *acting* like Tsars.

Communist rhetoric was that Ukraine was free, happy, and prosperous. For Ukrainians, the bitter truth was that Ukrainians harvested wheat and fought as soldiers for Russia. Ukraine, along with all the Sputnik Soviets, served Russia's interests. The true Ukrainian was still running from the Iron Wolf, hiding away among the hovels of the poor, constantly pursued and never at rest.

## Key Takeaways

- Cultural elements have been regarded as peripheral by Russia, but as essential by Ukrainians.
- Ukrainians told coded folk tales about the Russians and other oppressive invaders.
- Russians have despised the Ukrainian language, while Ukrainians resisted being made to speak Russian.
- Changes in the way news was spread made it impossible for Russia to make sure only the Russian viewpoint on Ukraine was expressed.

- Monuments built by pro-Russian officials in Ukraine are viewed with deep dislike by Ukrainian nationalists.

Russians tend to see themselves as Ukraine's benefactor, while Ukrainians tend to see Russia as another oppressor, because the Russian-dominated government of pre-1991 Ukraine did not pursue the freedom and self-determination of Ukraine.

Every aspect of Ukrainian culture is interpreted in diametrically opposite ways by official Russia and popular Ukraine. Those interpretations drive the political attitudes and actions of the opposing parties. This signals to us that we should be deeply suspicious of our own side's media, particularly if our own leaders are apparently infallibly successful, and nothing bad ever seems to happen in our country. We need to learn how to really read the press.

Our journey thus far has taken us from the Viking longboats on the Dnieper, through a dispiriting picking of our way through the smoke and chaos of eight centuries of warfare, to the brink of the next crisis. In the final three chapters, I want to analyze *what* has happened in order for us to better understand *why* war has once again become the "only option" for settling differences of opinion over Ukraine.

# PART 3. UKRAINE—WAR AGAIN

(Tong, 2022)

# Chapter 10. Russia Sets Its Pieces

(van 't Einde, 2021)

*"Whether you like it or not, history is on our side. We will bury you!"* —Khrushchev (1956)

War involves real deaths of many real people, and leaves incurable loss and anguish in its wake. Chess serenely follows specific and unalterable rules, whereas war is waged by deception and cheating. Chess pits two sides with identical resources—16 pieces—against each other. Chess is played on 64 squares, whereas war can engulf the world.

A lot of staring at the board and placing of pieces happened before the first salvo of Putin's "special military operation" in 2022. The great game of war starts long before the clock is started. The first pawns are in motion before the audience have even taken their seats, and before the press have unpacked their cameras and microphones. The world always wakes up to a war already in progress.

In this chapter, I am going to show which pieces Russia put in place before the conflict.

### Media Chum: Russia Sets the Mood for War

Shark cage diving operators prepare for their clients to see lots of sharks by chucking out a bucket of fish scraps, in a process called "chumming." In the same way, it makes the public more likely to tolerate your mood if you first stir up a frenzy in preparation for war.

Putin has been laying a base for Russians to accept his re-colonizing Ukraine for many years. He continued with the old invective against Ukraine as unstable, unruly, ungrateful, and dangerous neighbors—not to mention dangerously sympathetic to NATO, the old foe of Russia.

The majority of the Russian population had to be won over. Generals are mobilized by politicians, and politicians have to be careful to prepare their fickle followers to approve of their actions, although Vladimir Putin has shown a Stalinesque skill in manipulating approval.

Even Putin, though, has to beware of the ambitions of his internal Communist Party competitors. The political leadership, therefore, also needs to be prepared for war. Every political leader under Putin has three difficult tasks—to not alienate the boss (extremely dangerous) and also to recruit support for the boss's schemes, while at the same time pleasing their own supporters.

So, the majority of the Russian population has to be convinced that war would be justifiable—or that it is not actually a war. The signs of this build-up have been clear, and secret services and journalists have been reading the signs in an analysis of Russian propaganda.

Propaganda is not as simple as it used to be. There are too many cracks through which to glimpse alternative points of view. However, news consumers can still either apply filters of their own, or live contentedly under filters imposed by their governments.

### *Personality in Power: Putin*

Putin has a global profile, instantly recognizable on the TV stations of the world. When he speaks, people listen. He has demonstrated his willingness to exert force—even nuclear force—to achieve his aims, and he maintains an unpredictable and inscrutable persona. He intimidates world powers, who fear that the former KGB operative might not be squeamish about the methods he employs. Russia is strong and is led by a horse-riding strong man.

### *Russia as the Slavic Policeman*

The USA claims responsibility for international justice and democracy as a justification for many of its military interventions. Russia does exactly the same, and neither side acknowledges the legitimacy of the other. They both claim the sheriff's star. For the average Russian, it's a no-brainer. *Obviously* Russia is the only credible major nation. The USA has repeatedly demonstrated its corrupt capitalism.

As a result, if Ukraine can't manage its own internal affairs, the way forward is for Russia to step in as policeman. Ukraine can manifestly not govern properly, and its current regime, instead of being grateful to Russia, has rebelled against the Soviet liberators, instigated by NATO, and fueled by a secret national Nazi agenda.

If you believe all this, then you cheer Putin on. He is the only world leader who has the interests of the Slavic nations at heart.

### *The New Svyatogor—the "Ukrainian Nazi"*

Normal human beings cannot stomach too much killing of people just for the sake of winning a war. It helps motivate troops if they are actually killing some sort of monster, instead. The Nazis were truly monstrous, and look, *they are alive again in Ukraine!*

*Svyatogor* is a classic mythical monster who haunts the edges of Russian imagination; a gigantic Ukrainian warrior. Children are discouraged from dangerous or antisocial behavior by the threat of *Svyatogor*. They are also taught that the time will come when the Russian hero will shut the giant into a stone coffin.

Is this the time to kill the monster we have been taught to fear since childhood?

In this regard, Putin might be able to ignore world opinion if he can ensure home-ground advantage. One aspect of his war-chumming messaging has been Putin's elevation of the WWII Red Army victory to national cult status. Russia has been carefully led to forget the horrors of Stalin, while having their memories of Hitler vividly refreshed. Fortunately for Putin's rhetoric, there are indeed a handful of neo-Nazis in Ukraine. It is a simple matter for a well run press to turn all Ukrainians into new *Svyatogor-Nazi* monsters.

## Developing a Pro-Russian Population Inside Ukraine

While we are farming with Vladimirs and Volodomyrs, I am reminded of that other Vlad: Vlad the Impaler, of Romania. Part of the vampire tradition his story spawned, is that vampires are supposed not to be able to enter a home *unless they are invited.* A student of history will observe that the *but you invited us* ploy has been used before by the Cossacks, Tsarist Russia, and the Bolsheviks. Vladimir Putin claims he *has* been invited, and that he *has* to enter Ukraine to protect persecuted Russians. *Our suffering brothers are calling us* has been a major theme in his public speeches.

### *Long-Term Infiltration*

By the incentivizing of Russians to settle in the Donbas region, and exporting or killing millions of Ukrainians, the proportion of Russians to Ukrainians has changed appreciably in favor of the Russians, who now make up about 17% of the population, and constitute a large majority in the far eastern provinces and Crimea.

From a tactical point of view, a pro-Russian population would be more likely to support troops on the ground. They would also be a natural resource for recruiting and operating an intelligence network. Additionally, they could provide a handy legitimation for invasion.

Russia is technically opposed to any nation being involved in the hostile takeover of another nation. As a permanent member of the UN Security Council, Russia is tasked with policing the conduct of world nations. As a result, Putin is constrained to provide some show of legality for an aggressive move on Ukraine, and his main argument is that Russia is defending democracy and self-determination of Russian neighboring states. He bases this on transmogrifying Russian-heavy Eastern Ukrainian provinces into independent nation-states.

Yeah, it does sound unlikely.

### *Far-Right Parties and the Revolution*

The majority of Russian speaking Ukrainians in the east tend to support parties that demonstrate a respect for Russian ties. The Party of Regions (now the Opposition Bloc), the Communist Party of Ukraine, and the Progressive Socialist Party all have moderately pro-Russian agendas. These are perfectly normal for a parliamentary democracy where anyone can express their opinion about the way forward for their country.

Where the Russian war-preparations come in is the heavy financial backing of radical organizations through Russian oligarchs over the past two decades. Military strategy recognizes that conflicting loyalties in the defending nation favor the invader. The most articulate Ukrainian secessionist players are actually numerically very small. The two most headline-grabbing separatist "youth" organizations are *Proriv* ("the Breakthrough"—founded in 2005) and the *Eurasian Youth Movement* (founded in 2002). They get only a couple of hundred supporters at protest marches, but in the Russian press they are made to look like a mass-uprising of the proletariat.

If there is a revolution of the people, then Russia is obliged to offer fraternal assistance.

### *Russian Orthodox Support of Ukrainian-Russian Separatism*

Putin's Russia has secured support for Russification of Ukraine from the Orthodox Church. For years, Patriarch Kirill, the Metropolitan of Moscow, has been talking about the Russians of Eastern Ukraine as being martyrs to a savage Ukrainian oppression. He publically sent the Russian army into Ukraine with his official blessing. For those who prioritize the authority of the church, this is strong pre-assault chumming of the headspace of Russians. In a strange inversion, the Communist Party of Russia has now become the godly option for those who wish to resist the godless West.

### Military Moves

### *Modernization of the Russian Army*

Putin's state-controlled media has spent the last 14 years telling the world how formidable the Russian army has become since his 2008 reforms. Under Putin, a new structure—with 160 smaller, more nimble, self-sustaining brigades—means that the military can be more quickly deployed, and in more effective combat configurations. The number of professional soldiers was reduced to a more focused one million men. On paper and on TV, it had become a hardened, highly trained, and superbly equipped fighting force, ready to meet any need of the *Rodina.*

Military experts around the world were fascinated to see how it would fare in actual fighting conditions. Ukraine was looking more and more like being the New Russian Army's first combat deployment since Crimea.

### *Encrypted Communications*

The Russian military developed a state-of-the-art encrypted communications system, *Era*. Operating via 3G/4G infrastructure, it is completely dark. The Russian military learned the lessons of the Nazi *Enigma* system during the Second World War. With *Era*, there was no way an enemy could get the jump on them by eavesdropping orders.

This hi-tech solution to battle-communication is essential for the sort of nimbleness that contemporary armies need. Effective communications are essential for applying maximum force to your enemy's maximum weakness.

### *The Hi-Tech T-14 Armata Battle Tank*

Another of Putin's New Russian Army innovations is the T-14 Armata Tank. This is a revolutionary upgrade on the cold-war era tanks. Costing about $4 million apiece, it is a marvel of contemporary deadliness. It can eat up the worst terrain at 90 kmph, and is good for a 500km round trip without refueling.

The T-14 has reduced the number of crewmen to three by an automatic cannon-loading system. Innovative layered armor technology gives it higher protection. A computer-driven anti-missile defense system, and a patent anti-radar system turn it into an unlikely seeming 48-ton stealth weapon. Operators no longer have to sit on top of the ammunition, and a flushing toilet further raises morale. It outmatches any tank Ukraine is likely to be able to throw at it, and under the wings of a beast like the T-14, a battalion of infantrymen would be unstoppable as they raced across the landscape.

### *Assemble Overwhelming Force*

Russia has learned from their humiliation in Afghanistan in the 1980s, and have moved toward becoming a professional army, rather than a mass of expendable peasants led by a mass of bureaucratic officers. The military has systematically drawn its recruits from among Russian citizens alone—in this "Patriotic War," Russia would have to do without her go-to army of Ukrainians.

Each battalion is a self-sufficient army with all the transport, artillery, tanks, air-support, and logistics to make it a self-contained battle unit. Forbes, the form-guide for warfare, reckons that at the end of 2021, Russia had 160 battalions in play, 120 of which were being brought toward Ukraine (Hambling, 2022). That means about three quarters of all Russia's forces were thrown into Putin's "special military operation."

### *Strategy—Obliterate and Liberate*

The standard USSR military doctrine was to suddenly flood the targeted territory with overwhelming force, and install and maintain a communist, Russian-friendly regime, using secret police to enforce compliance and state-run media to unrelentingly thank Russia for liberation. Any questioning of the sociology of invasion, especially using a Marxian critique, is 100% banned.

RIA Novosti, the Moscow-based news outlet, is unapologetically open about the Russian objectives in Ukraine. After winning control by military means, Russia will dismantle the Ukrainian Army, establish Russian-controlled police and civic authorities, edit the libraries, and erect proper Russian statues, while introducing a 25-year plan to eliminate Nazis.

Ukraine, and the world, knew exactly what was coming. It felt like Stalin all over again.

### Key Takeaways

- The whole weight of Russian-controlled media was thrown behind persuading Russians to accept the justice of the annexation of Ukraine.
- Vladimir Putin is deliberately projecting a similar approach to leadership as Joseph Stalin.
- Putin uses the perceived threat of NATO to unite opinion against Ukraine.
- Russia has worked hard to promote divisive sentiment within Ukraine.
- Russia overhauled its military and invested heavily in new military equipment.
- Russia assembled a massive force close to the borders of Ukraine in 2021.

If your core tactic is total domination, you have to have the military force to back it up.

There are clues as to what Putin's next invasion plans are, based on the nature of his propaganda invective. Is he demonizing any other specific nations or people groups? Are the complaints and threats about Finland and Sweden joining NATO a clue as to where he will strike next?

Is Putin planning to reunite the old Soviet Union? It appears so.

Russia's build-up to invasion followed the usual planning steps, preparing home audiences and international audiences for the inevitable outcome. Because Russian preparations are so predictable, Ukraine was able to place specific pieces in specific places to counter the Russian plan.

It appears that Ukraine *did* prepare with the Russian "game" in mind. In the next chapter, I will consider how Zelensky's build-up to being invaded in 2022 proactively prepared for the coming storm.

# Chapter 11. Ukraine Sets Its Pieces

(Ehrhardt, 2015)

*Si vis pacem, para bellum ("if you want peace, prepare for war") –General Publius Flavius Vegetius Renatus* (Gill, 2019)

Sometimes, one team excels for so long that it appears nobody can ever beat them. Manchester United, in *English* "football," used to be invincible. But other teams studied the "Man-U" brand and playbook, and developed competitive strategies, brought in stellar managers and hyper-talented players, and suddenly Manchester United had become a mid-table team, with Manchester City precariously on top.

For two decades, it seemed that the team with Tom Brady as quarterback would be guaranteed a Super Bowl spot (in *American* "football"). A new crop of players are studying to bring his reign to an end, since he seems so unwilling to retire! Unequaled success calls out unparalleled effort, and eventually the mightiest fall.

Russia has done the same thing over and over again with regard to her troublesome southern province/southern neighbor, and run her standard invasion play over many other territories as well. The question I am asking in this chapter is, has a country—Ukraine to be specific—now managed to produce a playbook that will bring about a different result?

Ukraine's preparations for this war have been... interesting.

## Media Chum: Ukraine Sets the Mood for Resistance

Ukraine has opted for an open media strategy; a difficult terrain to master, with constantly shifting best practice. Regimes resort to bots to churn out a relentless storm of online propaganda, as do resistance movements. Their avatars then struggle for cyber control. The status quo might stay unchanged, but each side has to keep up to date, so as not to let the balance shift in the opposition's favor.

During the 2014 Russian "liberation" of Crimea, the Ukrainian government realized that it had to do something to counteract the Russian media supremacy in the region. The government banned anybody involved in government at any level and from any party from founding a press outlet, and enforced funding transparency. In 2020, they criminalized "fake news." In addition, there was a significant migration of public engagement to social media platforms. Ukrainians are not having to absorb a Russian diet of information, although they can if they want to.

This leveled the playing field somewhat, and pro-Ukrainian ideas did not have to covertly embed themselves in folk tales—they could now name the Iron Wolf.

There are three "media audiences": My state, the other state, and the world. Ukraine is up two-one on that score card.

### *Personality in Power: Zelensky*

In the lead-up to the 2022 invasion of Ukraine, a widely popular president rose to power, a man with a unique capacity to read audiences and motivate followers—Volodymyr Zelensky.

*Ukrainian, but not too Ukrainian.* Volodymyr Zelensky is a Russian-speaking Ukrainian from central Ukraine, a Jewish descendant of the decimated Jewish clans. He did not make his name as a Russian separatist or a Ukrainian politician. He is famous for being funny.

*Lovable comedian.* When Zelensky ran for president in 2019, people thought it was a publicity stunt for his show, in which he played an astonishingly inept ordinary citizen who accidentally became President of Ukraine. He had also dubbed the voice of Paddington Bear for the Ukrainian release, and in 2006 he won "Dancing with the Stars." He was an "A-list personality." And then he won the election!

*Reader of audiences.* Velensky's ability to relate to audiences is so rare among politicians that anyone who has the skills is sneered at as a "populist." But his acting skills were in place for phase two of the Russian invasion, and that was to give Ukraine a distinct advantage. Putin, on the other hand, has one persona—*How can I make you afraid of Russia*?

*Deliverer of punchlines*. Zelensky has the comedian's capacity to read a monologue well—and hit his punchlines unerringly—unlike the dreary rambling and stilted delivery that often passes for orthodox political oratory. He knows how to *sound* genuine, which contrasts sharply with the clichéd tone that characterizes Russian propaganda.

And he knows how to be *inspirational*, as this extract from his inaugural speech shows:

> *"We are all Ukrainians. There's no less of a Ukrainian or more of a Ukrainian, the right Ukrainian or wrong Ukrainian, we are all Ukrainians. From Uzhhhorod to Luhansk, from Chernihiv to Simferopol, in Lviv, Kharkiv, in Donetsk, Dnipro, and Odessa - we are all Ukrainians. We have to be united, and only then are we strong"* (McCallig, 2022).

It might turn out that Volodymyr Zelensky is the most important asset Ukraine had in place before the 2022 Russian invasion.

## Developing Ukrainian Nationalism

## *Politics Minus Crimea and Donbas*

The Russian re-acquisition of Crimea in 2014 resulted in large gains for Ukrainian political parties. Since Crimea had declared independence, its largely Russian citizens could no longer vote in Ukraine, which meant that the political landscape swung much further *for* Ukraine and *against* Russia.

During the 2014 elections, the Russian language political party, the *Petro Poroshenko Bloc,* made huge strides in Southern Ukraine, running on a "Ukrainian Russians for Ukraine" ticket. The *Ukrainian Communist Party* was eliminated due to a lack of support. The pro-Russian *Opposition Bloc* came in last. It became clear that Russian Ukrainians in Ukraine, exposed for the first time to other-than-state media, were also tending to choose Ukrainian self-determination.

The battle for political opinion had been a key pre-conflict piece put in place by the Ukrainians. There was more cross-party solidarity than ever before. The vast majority of Ukrainian politics was now united by the idea of an independent Ukraine.

## *More to Lose: The Education of Ukrainian Peasants*

Another political piece that was falling into place was the general boost to the economy that resulted in more people having more to lose. It was not that Ukraine was doing well, but rather that all resources were now being plowed straight back into developing the country. Now a sense of ownership and agency was emerging with a flavor similar to that of those early Vikings.

What Ukraine had managed to put on the board was an active, nationalistic population, more united than ever before, and highly articulate—at home and abroad—about their feelings about Russia. The middle class has more to lose, and more resources to keep what they had.

### *The Euromaidan Movement*

In 2014, the pro-European Euromaidan uprising shook the pro-Russian Ukrainian government of president Yanukovich, causing deep concern in Russia. Anything calling itself a "spontaneous revolution of the people" challenges the communist "rule of the people by the people." Revolutions sympathetic to the Euromaidan movement across the Slavic world were abruptly crushed. About 100 protesters were shot in Kyiv, which became ungovernable. The government folded, and Yanukovich went into exile. Pro-Russian counter-protests emerged.

Then, in March 2014, Russia annexed Ukraine.

Let's leave it there, because it was at around this time that the *preparations* for war merged into war itself.

## Military Moves

As the ever-moving chess board was set for this latest contestation of the land, Ukraine was putting military pieces in place. The arithmetic was grim: A population of 44 million against 160 Russian battalions. Russia had 35,000 troops permanently stationed on the Ukrainian border, and the capacity to swiftly bring another 150,000 into play. If you are in a David versus Goliath scenario, it is wise to pick up enough river stones for your sling, because Goliath is very big.

### *A Large Standing National Army*

The maxim of the Roman general Vegetius—preparing for war in order to ensure peace—was in full force in Ukraine, which had built up a large standing army, second only to Russia's in the region, consisting of over a quarter of a million personnel. If it had been a medieval war, with battalions facing off on a flat plain, it might have been close.

The difference was equipment. Russia had newer tanks and more tanks, better airplanes and more airplanes, vast stock-yards filled with armored personnel carriers, missile launchers, and a huge navy. Russia did not mind the satellite images of the swift accumulation of their troops. It was part of their "obliterate and liberate" strategy to evoke fear, just as it was part of their diplomatic strategy to deny any intention of invasion.

All Ukraine had was a home-ground advantage in occupation of terrain and morale. It remained to be seen how that would stand up against the heavy pieces being drawn up against them.

### *Trained Local Militias*

The memory of what victorious Russian forces have done in the past fuelled the recruitment of Ukrainian militias. An essential part of the peaceable Russian rule is the killing and imprisonment of anybody who has shown any resistance. This makes your chances of survival much higher, if you beat off the attack in the first place.

Ukraine armed 130,000 local militia fighters, trained to conduct hit-and-run raids on the flanks of what was expected to be an invading juggernaut. Large armies are vulnerable in many small places, although it takes many wounds to stop them. Ukraine was also developing strategies for enabling their standing forces to resist, hit, and defeat the enemy.

### *Hi-Tech Army*

The Ukrainian militias were armed with scraps and relics. Most of their stock was Russian, from the hardy AK47 to the still-functional Simonov AVS-36 (the name gives their original date of deployment—1936). The standing forces, however, were reasonably well armed, with the locally produced Zbroyar Z-15 as their standard assault rifle.

The Ukrainian army had been buying as much up-to-date hardware as they could. In 2016, they ordered Desert Tech SRS sniper rifles from the USA, followed by a big order for

Savage Arms 10BA sniper rifles. Along with their own locally manufactured Snipex T-Rex, it was obvious they were not setting the pieces in place for a toe-to-toe tank campaign. The Ukrainian army was desperate to fight on their own terms.

### *Strategy for Tanks*

Whether or not Trump wanted anything when dealing with the Ukrainian President Valodomyr Zelensky in the 2019 *do us a favor, though* phone call (the basis for President Trump's first impeachment hearing), it is completely clear what Zelensky wanted. He wanted Javelins. He kept slipping it in there.

In the same way that the longbow changed medieval war at Agincourt, the Javelin missile threatens to upset the old war paradigm that was based on the might of the battle tank. The Javelin is light, and can be carried by a team of two (one, if necessary) on foot. If the gunner can get a visual lock on the target from four kilometers away, he can let off a shot and then scramble for cover. Meanwhile, the missile guides itself to rear up and then attack the top-armor of the tank, at its weakest. In 2018, Ukraine got its first consignment of 37 launchers and 210 missiles. It wanted many more!

As the Trump phone call illustrates, Zelensky was desperate to stockpile Javelins. Ukraine's tactics were to fight from as far away from their invaders as possible.

Volodymyr Zelensky played his high profile in Western media to the maximum, as a good comedian-politician ought. Generally, when Russia takes a bite off a small neighboring country, the world hardly notices, treating it as part of the rhythm of life, like floods, tornadoes, and elections. Ukraine noted how apathetic the world response had been when Russia took Crimea.

By 2022, Zelensky had changed that around. The phone call to Trump in 2019 was a media coup for Ukraine. Uncomfortable as it was, Zelensky himself emerged with his reputation unscathed, and suddenly everybody in the Western press was discussing arms sales to Ukraine. Ukraine, armaments, and the threat facing the region spent many news cycles in the "breaking news" chiron.

Zelensky got a lot of sympathy. His comic-president to real-president story became a very newsworthy narrative. He came over as an affable, reasonable man who was good at dancing and comedy, and all sorts of things that people in the Western world could relate to. Putin was taciturn, menacing, and unreadable. Zelensky would always win the popularity prize.

By the time the inevitable warfare broke out, Zelensky had won the international media war. There would be no traction for *Pravda* and company to put much positive spin on their actions. Ukraine propaganda had crushed it!

**Key Takeaways**

- Ukraine prepared for 2022 by running an aggressive pro-Ukrainian propaganda campaign globally and in Ukraine itself.
- The election of Volodomyr Zelensky brought a man into power that the West could relate to.
- Politics in Ukraine switched strongly over to a Ukrainian self-determination agenda, across all parties.
- A rising middle-class made a stronger base for resistance to invasion.
- Pro-EU and pro-NATO agitation began in Ukraine and spread over the entire Slavic Bloc.
- Ukraine prepared for invasion by developing a large standing army, training and equipping local militias, and investing heavily in new hi-tech weaponry.

The Ukraine versus Russia conflict was heavily weighted in Russia's favor, by military standards. However, Ukrainian nationalism was at an all-time high. Freedom of the media and the history textbooks developed Ukrainian self-confidence. In addition, international opinion was seen to carry far more weight than it ever has, and new technology promised new solutions to tactical dilemmas.

Once everything is in place, the game must either be abandoned or begun. Ukraine was hoping against hope that having prepared for war, they would have peace. The Russian machine, impervious to the concerns and objections of Ukraine or the watching world, simply kept on course.

# Chapter 12. Tanks versus Drones in a "Tiktok War"

(WikiImages, 2012)

*"Putin wants to restore the Old Russian Empire and cannot stand free democratic prospects in Ukraine, because sooner or later the people of Russia would want to have that kind of lifestyle as well." –John McCain, 2014* (McCain, 2021)

This is the crossover where historian meets journalist in the jolting realities of the present. I have no idea of how things will turn out in the bruised wheatfields of Ukraine. This chapter investigates the interaction between long drawn up forces, as they play out on the "chessboard."

Future historians will scrutinize and evaluate my understanding, but we cannot wait for the future. This chapter records how the first pawns were moved in the latest game. Further phases will be reported by other journalists. The end game will come and go, and wise chess analysts will debate the strengths and weaknesses of the moves.

The ground I will cover in this last chapter is the way hostilities began, and how they started to develop in the Russian invasion of Ukraine in 2022.

Russia hungers after Ukraine with a deep, possessive yearning. In Putin's mind, and in the consciousness of countless Russians, Ukraine is not *meant* to be independent.

Ukraine is passionately conscious of its own independent identity, and feels chafed by eight centuries of shackles. Zelensky-led Ukraine sees itself as the independent corner shop that will not sell out to make way for the shopping mall.

## Ukrainian Invasion—Beta Test Crimea 2014

The first moves in this 2022 conflict were made in 2014, when Russia facilitated the secession of the Ukrainian province of Crimea and the establishment of two break-away republics from the east of Ukraine, the Luhansk People's Republic, and the Donetsk People's Republic. The global community hardly blinked an eye at the time. France and Germany did help broker a shaky peace, but the UN had been formed to stop acts of global aggression like this from happening.

Imagine Wisconsin and Minnesota declaring their independence, and then with the help of 5000 Canadian troops, establishing a hard border between themselves and the rest of the US, and then declaring that they will now pay federal taxes to their natural partners to the north, in the Union of Maple-Syrup Producers.

Ludicrous? That is what Crimea, Luhansk, and Donetsk did in 2014.

***Lightning Strike***

Russia took control of Crimea with fewer than 20,000 soldiers. They rolled in with almost no opposition, and when the dust had settled, Crimea "belonged" to Russia again.

This is how it went down.

Pro-Russian demonstrations erupted in the port city of Sevastopol in February 2014. Anonymous Russian troops (not very many) swooped in and took control of government and media infrastructure. Then, with very little opposition, they took over all the main centers in the peninsula and installed a pro-Russian administration under Sergey Aksyonov. By the end of March, there had been a referendum on incorporation into Russia (Yes, yes, yes, said everybody), and sweet as a nut, the "Republic of Crimea" and the "Federal City of Sevastopol" were federal partners/subjects of Russia. Putin rejects the label "annexation"—as he tells it, Russia won fair and square on overwhelming public opinion. Minnesota separatists should be glad to hear this—all they need to do is win a state-wide referendum of separation.

The USSR was taking shape once again. Putin threatened nuclear action, and everybody piped down. Nuclear deterrence deterred the invaded from protesting, and discouraged anybody from trying too hard to rescue Crimea from the Iron Wolf.

### *Model Battle Plan for Attack on Ukraine*

Everything had worked like clockwork. An internal cry had arisen from oppressed workers (Russian speaking, but Ukrainian Russians). Russia had liberated them from the Nazi NATO-backed and Europe-sympathizing grip of Kyiv.

Russia immediately ramped up support for separationist movements in Eastern Ukraine. Its modus operandi was simple to understand but hard to resist, much like the strategy of the Springboks in playing Rugby. Power trumped weakness, and rhetoric trumped subtlety.

### *A Bridge Too Far?*

As a military move, the annexation of Crimea was admirable and efficient. As a step toward taking the whole of Ukraine, however, it might turn out to have been self-defeating.

Ukraine before Crimea was deeply troubled, crime-ridden, and corruption plagued. Dissatisfaction with the old way of ruling was riding high, and the West—and all things Western—were becoming more and more alluring to the population as a whole. As McCain noted in the epigraph to this chapter, you don't want your people to even *see* the greener grass. Once they see it, it's hard to convince them that Euro-grass is bad compared to the brown, withered Russian-grass.

A far-reaching aspirational movement was developing. Ukrainian nationalism became a notional tool for leaving the Russian East and joining up with the European West. Anti-Russian solidarity was ratcheted up a notch. Anyone could see that Putin wanted the *whole* of Ukraine. In 2021, he even wrote an essay (well, probably his ghostwriter did) in which he argued that Russians and Ukrainians were "one people" (Putin, 2021). For anyone who had managed to get a reliable history text on the Stalin years, this would have been horrifying.

At just the wrong time for Russian plans, Ukrainian self-consciousness reached its highest level in eight centuries. The mood of the nation crystallized as needing to move away from Russia, and toward Europe under the powerful leadership of Zelensky.

A seemingly easy pacification of a sympathetic region (Crimea) might just be the spark that ignited an explosion of resistance in Ukraine.

## The Post-Covid Invasion of Ukraine

Putin used the 2014 playbook on Crimea again in 2022. He simply cut and pasted—I suppose he thought *why fix something that isn't broken?* This time, the "invitation" came from pro-secessionist groups among the Russian-speaking population of Eastern Ukraine. The chatter from *Proriv* and the *Eurasian Youth Movement* (they of the 100-man "mass protests") was that they were being repressed by a horrific neo-Nazi zombie state, and needed liberation.

The self-declared independent statelets of Donetsk and Luhansk started mobilizing forces on February 19th, 2022. On February 21st, Putin sent troops and military equipment to back them in their revolution. On February 24th, the Russian tanks rolled into Ukraine, and the war began.

This time it did not go to plan.

## The Battle for Kyiv

### *Kyiv in Three Days, Ukraine in a Week*

A poignant story in the Western news is that the one item found in every dead Russian soldier's battle pack was their ceremonial uniforms for the victory parade in Kyiv—"the day after tomorrow." Whether or not that is propaganda, there have not been any victory parades yet. *Pravda* has not been able to show Russian battle tanks riding in triumphant formation under the stern gaze of the *Rodina Mat* monument. Halfway through 2022, the Russians have been struggling for months to bring the great weight of the Russian army to bear on their pesky little opponent.

The Russians were beaten back from Kyiv. There is talk of tanks running out of gas, logistic support columns stranded and captured, and general disorganization and mayhem.

Ukrainians claim lots of Russian tanks have been blown up by their Javelins. The Russians claim that is a great exaggeration. The truth is that although the countryside is burned and broken, the Russians have abandoned their "lightning push" on Kyiv, pulling back to fight an easier, long-haul war on the open plains of the east. It has become clear that the old Soviet style approach of sending in massive waves of tanks and troops has been effectively countered by Ukraine's new technology.

### The Battle for Kherson

In 988 CE, Vladimir the Great sacked Cherson. In 2022, Vladimir the Recent sacked it again, under its new name of Kherson.

On March 2nd, Russian forces, massed in Crimea and then moving north, quickly overran Kherson. It was an encouragement to the Russian cause, and the *Pravda* celebrations made up for the missing celebrations over Kyiv. Kherson and Kyiv were two key points that were meant to fall in a swift pincer movement. Unfortunately for the Russian cause, the pincers broke, leaving them with the lesser prize of Kherson. The Ukrainians have sniped back, but their military doctrine does not envisage pitched battles with entrenched enemies.

From the Ukrainian point of view, it is indeed a significant loss, and it demonstrates the imbalance of power between the two militaries. Ukrainian hope lies in making a long-term occupation untenable. Even *Pravda* will find it hard to spin years of resistance into a happy welcome of liberators.

## The Battle for Mariupol

Russian forces quickly overran the Southern Ukrainian industrial city of Mariupol, but a group of Ukrainian soldiers retreated to the Azovstal steelworks and held out against everything the Russians could throw at them. Spring faded into summer, and in May, the Ukrainians were still entrenched at Azovstal. Mariupol has been a disaster for the Russian propaganda machine. A group of hard-bitten heroes fighting to the death *in a steel mill* is exactly what they would *not* have wanted—it is *bad* press. There is no question that Russia effectively controls the city they have invaded, but it has lost time, reputation, and a significant number of personnel in mopping up the last of the resistance.

From a purely arithmetical point of view, though, Mariupol is another major loss for the Ukrainian side. The Russian forces have now opened up a broad path from Moscow to the sea. If Russia can hold it (and Stalingrad reminds us they are very good at holding positions), then it leaves Ukraine much weakened.

## The Battle for the Donbas

The Battle for the Donets Basin region (known as "the Donbas") is a move by Russia to complete the stranglehold on the industrial economy of Ukraine. As I write, this has been half secured by Russia. Their plan is obviously to liberate the region, and establish pro-Russian communist governments that will subject themself to a reborn USSR.

I am not sure how a lightweight Ukrainian fighter can defeat the old heavyweight Russian wrestler here. Perhaps the battle will have to be fought elsewhere, on a battlefield of politics and global opinion?

Or Zelensky might have a surprise in reserve?

## Political Operations

Putin has been fomenting a cult of Russia's prowess in WWII, grooming the Russian public for further liberationist warfare. What Putin needed from the Ukraine invasion was a quick triumph and a sense (back in Russia) that Vladimir Putin had restored the world to what it should be, vindicating communism's ideological supremacy, Russia's indomitable military, and the inevitability of Putin's continued hold on power.

If the first two were shaken, then Putin's grasp of power would be threatened. The Ukraine offensive *had* to go well. It has not.

### *Putin's Special Military Operation*

Putin's media strategy team had a delicate operation in hand.

On the one hand, a breathtakingly swift four day campaign would make excellent propaganda. It could be spun as a demonstration of the great relief with which Ukrainians had welcomed their Russian liberators, and how little resistance the neo-Nazi ruling cabal had been able to muster. The voice of the people of Ukraine was one of gratitude to Russia, and delight in joining a new version of the USSR in achieving prosperity, peace, and progress. Power to the people.

A key element in this intended message was that this was no "war" or "invasion." It was simply a "special military operation" designed to facilitate a little re-adjustment in international relations between Ukraine and Russia. It had worked so well in Crimea, after all.

On the other hand, the Russian public would not approve of a bloody and protracted conflict with a neighboring state. They might sympathize with Putin's rationale, but once you began to cremate too many young Russian soldiers, it would be difficult to paint the operation as glorious and victorious.

### *Bots and the Battle for Media Supremacy*

Ukraine has tried to match every move made by Russia over the last ten years. My social media feed suggests that there is nothing but Zelensky out there, and that everyone in the world is hostile to the Russian invasion of Ukraine.

It may seem so. But *Roskomnadzor*, the efficient Russian censorship organization, has closed down access to Meta (Facebook and Instagram) for its own citizens. That leaves Russians to state media, which are relentlessly pro-Putin, and to Russian social media platforms *Odnoklassniki* and

*Vkontakte*, which means, among other things, that the income stream of a host of young influencers has come to a screeching halt. It could be that the vast majority of Russians are backing Putin's Ukrainian special military operation to the hilt. Or not. Gallup is not able to do any polls in Russia!

### *Zelensky on TikTok*

Consider this line of data:

> v.zelensky1 ZelenskyUA 12.6K views 1.9K Likes, 8 Comments. TikTok video from ZelenskyUA (@v.zelensky1): "UA#ukraineUA #zelensky #ukraine #slavaukraine". Another love. UA #ukraineUA #zelensky #ukraine #slavaukraine

It's information from a pro-Zelensky TikTok account. Vladimir Putin also has his TikTok accounts. It is a sign of our times that the premiers of two opponents in a ground war should both embrace a website famous for teenagers doing cool dance moves. Each of them, in their own way, needs all the support they can get. If only they could compete in a dance off and avoid all those thousands of deaths.

But then, Zelensky would almost certainly win. He can do live appearances on vast online screens at award ceremonies in the USA. Putin cannot. A man like Putin could neither accept such a challenge, nor accept such an outcome.

## Glitches in the Russian War Machine

Military commands do not want to tell the truth about their successes and losses, unless they are having a lot of success. Nothing is published that might help the enemy. And yet—it does seem that there must be severe problems with the Russian military machine. For all its preparedness and clever use of hi-tech resources, nobody would have thought that a little, under-resourced and internationally isolated country like Ukraine would have been able to stand up to the Russian behemoth for so long.

Some trends are emerging that might explain the situation.

### *No New Tanks*

First off, Russia has not been able to deploy the much vaunted new T-14 Armata Tank. Russian media have been boasting about it for a long time, but there are only about 20 in existence. The long lines of tanks we see in Pravda's coverage are almost all T-72 tanks with their 50-year-old design, which features no flushing toilet, and whose crew must still sit on top of the ammunition. Many of them are extremely elderly vehicles. The mind boggles at engineers trying to coax their old machines to turn up on time at the battlefield.

### *Communications Failures*

One of the most gobsmacking reports from the battlefields of Ukraine is that as the Russian Army has advanced, they have systematically destroyed cell-phone towers, because of all the potential they offer for communications between their enemies on the ground. Unfortunately, their state of the art encrypted communications system, *Era*, works off 3G/4G networks. Oops.

The story is that the Russian communications have been talking to each other via unencrypted radios, and Ukrainian ham radio operators are easily able to intercept their conversations. The degree of disorganization and lack of coordination made evident in the Kyiv debacle suggests that this might indeed be a crippling factor in their plans.

### *The Problem of Drones*

It seems that Russia is not using drone technology much in Ukraine. They did do so in the annexation of Crimea in 2014, but this 2022 operation seems to have been oddly old-school.

Ukraine, on the other hand, has invested heavily in drones. Its go-to killer is the Turkish Bayraktar TB2, which can knock out a tank. Ukraine also appears to be using modified off-the-shelf drones to good effect for surveillance. And the USA has promised supplies of its tiny but deadly Switchblade "kamikaze" drones.

This would explain the pictures of smoldering tanks that have been filling Western media. Bomb-carrying drones combined with four-kilometer-ranged Javelin missiles would explain why the armored push on Kyiv faltered and failed.

### *The Moskva*

Russia has one of the most powerful navies in the world. It is hard to explain, then, how a country with *no ships at all* could sink the *Moskva*, the most advanced guided missile cruiser of the Russian fleet.

Ukraine had lost all its navy when the Russians took over Sevastopol in Crimea. The naval assault from Russia was therefore unchallenged. Led by the flagship *Moskva*, their undisputed superiority on the sea facilitated the early successes of Russia in the south-east of the country.

*Moskva* was a public relations marvel—protected by the latest anti-missile technology. To make assurance doubly sure, it carried an ultra-rare and very holy relic from the Orthodox Church—a fragment of the true cross of Christ. I find that a little bewildering, this being the world's leading communist power, where religion is routinely derided. I suppose sailors are superstitious, though, and the authorities felt they should be humored.

However, there must be some doubt about the authenticity of the relic. The Ukrainians slipped a couple of R-360 Neptune anti-ship missiles into her, and she sank in the Black Sea.

### *High Casualty Count*

Too many Russian soldiers are getting killed in action. That may sound odd, since armies characteristically regard soldiers as expendable pawns. According to *Russian* military media, however, on *one weekend* recently they lost 800 men, and evacuated 1,600 wounded soldiers, along with the loss of "62 tanks, 101 armored personnel carriers, 129 vehicles, 24 artillery pieces, 8 anti-aircraft batteries, 7 airplanes, and 40 killer drones" (Atlamazoglou, 2022).

That is not to say that the Ukranians haven't suffered losses. They are admitting to 3000 killed and 10,000 wounded for the war so far, but, as with the Russians, that is a debatable military wartime report. The issue is, *many* Russian soldiers *have* been killed or wounded.

I do not think that the generals expected to take on so many casualties. And speaking of generals, it appears that the Ukrainians have developed a way of reaching those who have traditionally been shielded by foot soldiers. Russia has reported the deaths of 40 high-ranking officers in Ukraine so far—Lieutenant Colonels and Generals and the like.

Perhaps if Ukraine can hold out against the odds for long enough, Russia might be forced to back down, unlikely as that might seem under Putin. If the war gets too costly, though, Putin will cease to be a factor.

### Weapons of a Postmodern World

The history of warfare is a history of changing weapon-systems and changing alliances. This is the first major global conflict to have free access to artificial intelligence technology. Where in the past a horseman would have to carry a saber into conflict and aim his slashes and thrusts manually, a hidden missile-carrying man can deliver a lethal blow from the edge of sight. The art of alliances is, however, still as important as ever it has been.

## *International Alliances*

All the NATO countries, and the majority of the UN signatories, have joined in a strong chorus of disapproval of Putin's Ukrainian invasion. There was a similar, although fainter, negative reaction when he took Crimea. Governments know that their people feel strongly sympathetic to Zelensky, and governments always need to please their people.

The Zelensky magic has conjured up an alliance with the world. Putin, on the other hand, is alone in this with Belarus. Putin is easily capable of choosing his own path, but the global solidarity forming behind Zelensky is a formidable wartime asset for a tiny country. The way Zelensky is playing his limited hand is that he wants Ukraine to be a neutral buffer-state between Russia and Europe; a sort of Eastern Switzerland. If he can pull this off, it will be of enormous benefit to Ukraine in the long run.

Putin wants land and people and control over the entire region. That increases the fear of Europe and the world. Zelensky's line, that if Ukraine falls, the rest of Europe could be next, is touching a chord among his supporters.

## *Weapons Deals and Gifts*

The global embrace of Ukraine's cause has resulted in a deluge of equipment being shipped into the war zone. The USA has sent plane-loads of Javelin missiles. Belgium has gifted 5000 assault rifles. Arms manufacturers are falling over each other to donate (and showcase) their weaponry. Netherlands, Germany, Spain, and Italy—all of NATO is arming Ukrainian forces.

This is both proving and producing what Putin has said, that Ukraine is a danger to Russia because of its ties with NATO. It makes a handy talking point for *Pravda*, and increases the dread among Putin's constituency. Fear makes an effective motivator of support, and both sides know its value. It also means, however, that Ukraine has had the firepower to resist and retard Russian moves on the ground.

## *Sanctions & the Power of Global Opinion*

There are a trickle of mercenaries from around the globe fighting on the ground in Ukraine, but the most devastating support from Ukraine's allies is a crushing embargo on Russia. Banking facilities in Russia have been revoked. Trade has come to a standstill, even with natural gas, Russia's last remaining chip to play. Russia struggles to find buyers for its oil, steel, or any other products. Heck, even McDonald's has shut down operations in Russia!

The country has been backed into isolation. Its sports people are being spurned. Medvedev, a brilliant tennis player with no connection to Putin's war, has been banned from the Wimbledon Tennis Tournament. It's not his fault—it's the "Russia" brand.

If Ukraine can hold out, the discomfort on ordinary Russians exerted by these sanctions might be enough to end the war in their favor. Putin is reciprocating by squeezing what he can out of occupied Ukrainian areas—agricultural equipment and grain shipments are leaving the area of Kherson for other regions of the curtailed Russian empire. People with the memory of the *Holodomor* are deeply troubled. Another way of reciprocation is Putin's declaration of his intent to push through his purposes by the use of nuclear weapons. This has always been a terrifying stick to wave, as people ask themselves how much Putin is prepared to lose to achieve his ambitions.

Putin might be able to coerce or manipulate the appearance of support. In the long run, however, Russian morale will be quickly sapped if its Western luxuries and necessities are curtailed for too long. *Is Ukraine really worth it*? people will start to say. By the looks of the clampdown on internal Russian dissent, it seems that process is well under way.

### *Hack Attack*

Indications are that both Russia and Ukraine are furiously trying to hack each other's systems. With an unseen army of extremely bright young minds, it must be an adrenaline filled space! The focus of Russian hacking has been to break down Ukrainian systems in conjunction with missile attacks. Ukrainian hackers are encouraged to excel, therefore, by the thought that the building they are sitting in might be actually blown to bits. This is real life *World of Warcraft,* only you never get a new life.

Where Ukraine has an advantage is in the sheer numbers of hackers aligned to their cause. This is warfare that can be launched from anywhere on the globe, and Ukraine has consciously targeted global support in this "cybermilitancy." The day after the Russian incursion, the Ukrainian Minister for Digital Transformation went online calling for "digital talents for the creation of an IT army" (SEIBT, 2022). Russian and Belarussian command and logistics systems have had to endure a barrage of irritating and damaging infiltrations by such attack-groups as *Anonymous*, *Squad303*, and *Cyber Partisan.*

The feared Russian hacking capability seems to have been outgunned in this arena in the early stages of the 2022 war. It is an interesting area to watch, and appears to be a crucial weapon in the arsenals of the two combatants.

**Key Takeaways**

- Russia began hostilities against Ukraine in 2014, when it took control of Crimea.
- The Russian justification for invasion was premised on a notional invitation for help from oppressed Ukrainian citizens.
- The Russians launched a major offensive against Ukraine in 2022, calling it a "special military operation."
- Russia failed to take the Ukrainian capital of Kyiv, but succeeded in taking the south-eastern cities of Kherson and Mariupol.
- Political propaganda strategies were ramped up by both sides.

- Russian forces were repulsed or stalled by problems with facing Ukrainian anti-tank capabilities, and their own infrastructure and support problems.
- High numbers of Russian and Ukrainian personnel were killed and injured. Curiously, a disproportionately high number of senior Russian officers were killed, including at least eight generals.
- Sanctions imposed on Russia proved to be a major obstacle to their war effort.
- Civilian casualties in Ukraine were also very high.
- Hacking proved to be a major new component of warfare.

Russia has a conscious strategy to divide and dominate its neighboring countries. The world needs to consider whether there is any limit to its ambitions. The 2022 conflict has shown that global warfare is at a technological turning point. New weapons can turn old advantages on their head.

Nonetheless, alliances are always critical in warfare. Peacetime should be largely devoted to making friends. Russia has not done this for a long time, and is demonstrably afraid of unified action against it, which means that the possibility of Ukraine joining NATO was one of the key triggers for this war. Gains for NATO are losses for a burgeoning neo-USSR.

That then, is where we have to draw the line under *history to this point*. The 2022 Russian invasion of Ukraine has not blown up out of nowhere. It is the latest in a long series of upheavals that has torn Ukraine down the centuries. As with all conflicts, however, people who wage them fight in the hope that *this* at last will be the “war to end all wars.”

# Conclusion—Vladimir versus Volodymyr

(Mediamodifier, 2022)

*"The fight is here; I need ammunition, not a ride." — Volodymyr Zelensky, when offered a safe place to rule Ukraine from exile* (McCallig, 2022)

The 2022 war on Ukraine can be boiled down to how the two protagonists read the history of Ukraine. The two Vladimirs (or the two Volodymyrs!) are cousins in culture. Their names betray their common ancestry. They share the same roots in the Vikings of the Dark Ages and the original Kyivan Rus'. But one culture has grown at the expense of the other. Ukraine has desperately held onto a secret independent identity while Russia has expanded its identity into a globe-dominating persona.

Investigating the chain of command in Ukraine shows that the people of the earth—the Ukrainian peasants—have had to serve Poles or Austrians or Cossacks or Mongols or Russians throughout most of their existence.

Putin appeals to the history of subjugation and exploitation of Ukraine as establishing Russian rights to the use of its "Ukrainian Province."

Zelensky, on the other hand, evokes memories of the Vikings who rowed down the Dnieper and established an independent marauder's kingdom.

The 2022 conflict is still in the balance. The history of Ukraine shows that it has *always* been in the midst of a crisis; always a place of unfinished business. There has never been a leisurely moment to look back on and ponder—the next armies are always arming for battle over Ukraine. I offer this journalist's view to help you make sense of what is happening and spot old trends—but also, hopefully, emerging trends that will allow history to take a different direction.

My hope is that reflection on this ugly war will offer us insights into how to make our world a more peaceful place.

THE END

# Appendix. Milestone Moments in History That Explain the 2022 Invasion

(Pilger, 2017)

*"War is like a game of chess... but with this little difference, that in chess a knight is always stronger than a pawn, while in war a battalion is sometimes stronger than a division and sometimes weaker than a company. Success never depends, and never will depend, on position, or equipment, or even on numbers, and least of all on position." —Leo Tolstoy*

Social media loves lists: Ten ways to lose weight; seven low-impact exercises; five hacks that will put you to sleep. I offer you here a list of 11 historical data points to understand the current Ukrainian war. What this list shows is that empires rise and fall in an unending struggle for advantage and domination. The answer to the "why" question seems to be that, as soon as nation states gain power and influence, they long for more. They gain "more" either by direct conquest or by forging alliances for mutual self interest. The 2022 invasion of Ukraine shows that Russia seeks to conquer while Ukraine seeks to ally itself with the Nato Bloc. To summarize—